Introduction to the Stamps of Mexico

By Dale Pulver

Published by *Linn's Stamp News*, the largest and most informative stamp newspaper in the world. *Linn''s is owned* by Amos Press, 911 Vandemark Road, Sidney, Ohio 45365. Amos Press also publishes *Scott Stamp Monthly* and the Scott line of catalogs and albums. Copyright 1992 by Linn's Stamp News. On the cover: An example of one of Mexico's Black Mulitas. Most experts say the Black Mulitas were prepared as a presentation set for the Universal Postal Union but were also given to the diplomatic corps and notable Mexican politicians. The stamps are identical to the regular stamps, except that all denominations are printed in black. The Black Mulitas are described on page 31. Cover design by Veronica Schreiber.

Contents

Contents

Introduction

By Michael Laurence

Dale Pulver's Mexico column has been a regular feature in *Linn's* for almost 10 years. Month after month, Pulver has provided *Linn's* readers with fascinating insights into the stamps and postal history of our neighbor to the south. Pulver's writing conveys his enthusiasm as well as his knowledge, and as a result, his *Linn's* column has developed a loyal following even among readers who don't have a collecting interest in the subject.

"I've never collected Mexico," one *Linn's* reader wrote us, "but I always read Dale Pulver's column because it's so interesting. I learn something new every time."

One of the great joys of Mexican philately is its diversity. As Pulver liked to say, Mexico contains something for everybody. Whether you're a one-of-each beginner looking to fill spaces in a newly acquired album, or an advanced specialist seeking a new area in which to form an international exhibition collection, the stamps of Mexico have much to offer.

Appropriately, the literature of Mexican philately is rich. But at least in the English language, the subject lacks an introductory overview. This work, based on a revision and reorganization of about 40 of Pulver's *Linn's* columns, is intended to fill that gap.

This is the third book in the *Linn's* Handbook series. The first is *Classic United States Imperforate Stamps*, by Jon Rose, published in 1990. The second is *United States Postal History Sampler*, by Richard B. Graham, published in 1991. The *Linn's* Handbooks are a continuing series of original works, in a common format, on a broad range of stamp collecting subjects, conceived, created and priced to be within the grasp of ordinary stamp collectors. The overriding objective of the series is to bring useful information to the widest possible audience.

Foreword

Dale R. Pulver began collecting stamps at age eight, when his aunt gave him a stamp album. This was the year 1937, and the definitive series of the Fourth Bureau issue was in the U.S. Post Office. Dale spent his youth collecting worldwide stamps until his interest was displaced by other worldly matters like school, marriage, family and early work responsibilities.

In 1964, Dale, by now a chemical engineer, was transferred to Mexico and, there, was introduced to Mexican philately. He attended the Efimex stamp show in Mexico City in 1968. The show hosted the annual convention of the Mexican Elmhurst Philatelic Society International (MEPSI). Though Dale had already acquired some Mexican pieces, the exhibits by notables, such as Jim Beal, Herbert Strauss, Otto Yag and others, spurred his interest. He became an avid collector of Mexico.

Dale joined MEPSI in 1966 and has supported its objectives since. He returned to the United States in 1969.

By the 1970s, Dale's philatelic experience had progressed to the point that he felt he had a need to share this experience with others. He did this by exhibiting extensively in the 1970s and 1980s. All of his exhibits featured some aspect of Mexican philately. He captured national grand awards at Indypex 85, Dayton 82, as well as two international awards. Themes of his exhibits included "First Design 1856, '61 and '67," "Forwarding Agents' Cachets on Mail To and From Mexico," "Mexican-American War 1846-48," "Mexican Revenues Up to 1914," "Mexican Monarchy Issues 1864-67," "The French-Mexican Connection" and stampless covers of Mexican philately.

As Dale's experiences increased, he began writing articles on Mexican philately in the 1970s. His articles in the U.S. Classics Society's *Chronicle*, won the Ashbrook cup in 1978. He was awarded the McCoy award in 1987 for his article on Mexican stampless covers in the *American Philatelic Congress* book. In 1983 he began writing a Mexico column for *Linn's*.

Dale graduated from Cornell University with a BS in chemical engineering in 1952. He retired after 34 years with Diamond Shamrock in 1986. He has been married 38 years to his wife, Christine, and has three children and four grandchildren. He spends most of his retirement days doing community volunteer work, working in his woodworking shop and studying philately. He is an active member of the Garfield-Perry Stamp Club of Cleveland and is a member of other philatelic societies.

I share Dale's interest in Mexican philately and believe it is the most interesting and aesthetically rewarding field of philately in the world. In Dale's 114 published columns on Mexico, he has covered almost all the aspects from prestamp postal history through the current Exporta definitives, postal stationery and related areas, such as official seals, tax stamps, TB seals and others.

Consolidation and publication of these articles in book form is certain to be a great service to those wanting to learn about collecting Mexican stamps. *Linn's Introduction to the Stamps of Mexico* will serve as a primer by making available basic information on the many aspects of Mexican philately, as well as warning the unwary of the many forgeries in the market.

As a friend of Dale's and a fellow collector of Mexico, I count my good fortune in knowing Dale Pulver. I find it an honor to be asked to write this foreword.

W.E. "Bill" Shelton

Chapter 1

Classic Era 1856-83

District overprints on 1856-61 issues

Mexico's first adhesive postage stamps appeared on August 1, 1856. This was 16 years after the famous Penny Black made its debut in Great Britain, and nine years after the United States issued its first postage stamps. But it was comfortably ahead of most of Mexico's Central American neighbors.

Five denominations made up the first issue: ½ real (blue), 1r (yellow), 2r (yellow-green), 4r (red) and 8r (lilac). There was a legitimate need for all these values since postage was based on weight and distance. The series provided the combinations necessary to match these scaled rates.

The common design of the five stamps pictured Miguel Hidalgo y Costilla, an early leader in Mexico's war for independence.

The stamps were engraved, well-executed and printed in attractive colors. However, early collectors found something curious about them — something they were unable to explain for many years. Nearly all of these stamps bore, in addition to cancellations, names such as those seen running vertically along the sides of the stamps in Figure 1. This pair of 1r stamps from the district of Mazatlan, used at Culiacan, shows the overprinted district name.

These names were neatly applied, for the most part. Anyone having a smattering of geographic knowledge about Mexico would assume they were towns and cities. Many had a common familiar ring to them — Mexico, Puebla, Acapulco, Veracruz and Tampico. Others were veritable tongue-twisters — Huejutla, Ixtlahuaca, Polotitlan, Soyaniquilpan, Temascaltepec and Tlalpujuahua. Some of the names were seen again and again; others were seldom encountered.

Before the turn of the century, when more and more of the early classic stamps of Mexico began appearing on the market, a British businessman named Samuel Chapman took keen interest in these markings and began the search for a logical explanation. At the time, Chapman was living and working in Mexico, which facilitated his studies immensely. He discovered that the names were district overprints, a clever system of security devised by the Mexican postal authorities. In the mid-19th century, Mexico was rife with social and political upheaval. It was also a country with a widely dispersed population, due to its rugged geography. Communications, even between major cities, were difficult.

There was a fairly well-ordered postal system. Much of its structure dated from the days of Spanish colonial rule. The country was divided into postal districts, each having at least a principal office

Figure 1. A pair of 1-real stamps from the district of Mazatlan used at Culiacan shows the overprinted district name.

1

and often many suboffices.

A district office would order stamps from the main office in Mexico City in accordance with estimated local needs. The stamps would be shipped unoverprinted, usually by stagecoach. Once the stamps were received at the district office, they were handstamped with that district's name to validate them for use. Properly overprinted and canceled stamps are shown in Figure 2.

Stamps lacking the district name were presumed to be without franking power. In this way, the government hoped to control the unauthorized use of stamps and loss of revenue in the event the stamps were stolen.

This is the way the postal directives read, but it didn't always happen this way. A number of offices misunderstood the directive or chose to ignore it. Thus, we have stamps legitimately used without overprints, some of which are quite rare.

Also, in offices that handled a great deal of mail, the chore of applying the name to hundreds of stamps was a tedious job, so a tired or distracted clerk might miss a stamp or two along the way. Because of this, stamps sometimes appear with no overprint but with a clear cancel from a district that normally overprinted its stamps. Figure 3 shows an example from either Huejutla or Tulancingo.

This should explain why the first issue of Mexico, and some of those immediately following it, are so popular with specialists. First, we have an attractive, well-executed series of stamps. Then we have some 50 different district offices that applied name overprints and a number of offices that didn't, creating distinct, collectible varieties.

Further, there were numerous small offices (subdistrict offices) that received stamps from the larger offices but used different cancellations to permit them to be identified. Finally, there is a normal complement of printing flaws and varieties, usages outside of districts, fancy cancellations, and fakes and forgeries. Examples of stamps used outside the proper district are shown in Figure 4.

Fortunately, the scholarly and always precise Chapman spent many years sorting out the details of these issues, using original post office records as the basis for his work. In 1926 he documented his labors in a classic reference work, *The Postage Stamps of Mexico 1856-1868.* It is still available in a reprinted version.

The book gives the relative scarcity of the stamps based on Chapman's tables of shipments to the various districts. Some values, particularly the 4r and 8r stamps, are exceedingly scarce for several districts. Even some small districts used so few of the common values (1r and 2r) that these stamps, too, are scarce.

The hunt for these scarce overprints is exciting, though often expensive. For examples bearing the more common district overprints, however, the Scott catalog prices for the first three stamps in the series are each $17.50 or less. In my opinion, this is still a big bargain in the area of classic stamps.

True, one will pay more for very fine copies if he is dealing with well-informed sellers or auction competition, and one cannot hope to assemble a representative collection without substantial outlay.

The numbers of stamps sold for Mexico Scott 1-3 were: ½r 992,000; 1r 1.43 million; and 2r 1.63 million — not an overwhelming emission by anyone's measure.

A few comments about the so-called 1861 issue are in order. While Scott and most other catalogs list as a separate issue the stamps of the first design that appeared in 1861 in different colors and on colored paper, it is doubtful that the Mexican post office considered it

Figure 2. Bull's-eye strikes of circular datestamps on stamps overprinted for the districts of Tampico and Morelia show the proper usage of the stamps. The dates are November 2, 1857 (top) and October 26, 1857 (bottom).

such. The same plates were used for the 1856 stamps, the postal districts were basically the same, and there was no break in the numbering of invoices at the main dispatch office.

Since these stamps were in use for only three years (until May 1864), they are correspondingly scarcer than the earlier set. But they never have been as popular as the 1856 stamps, perhaps because the plates were wearing and the printing quality was inferior. The colors were not that attractive.

The acquisition of good, clear specimens provides a real challenge, particularly for the 1r and 2r, which appear fuzzy or blurred because of the condition of the plates. Use of a softer, thin wove paper was another new wrinkle that contributed to poor stamp quality.

The 1861 stamps were used until the early summer of 1864. The last shipment invoice to a Mexican post office was dated May 9.

Eagle series: first issue of the monarchy, 1864-66

Mexican specialists refer to the 1864-66 stamps (Scott 18-25) as the Eagles, although they are more properly called the first issue of the empire. This issue has always been a favorite of mine, although I haven't collected it extensively. The central design is the Mexican coat of arms showing an eagle perched on a cactus and holding a serpent in its mouth. But the eagle wears a crown.

The historical backdrop to all this was the attempt by certain Mexicans and Napoleon III, emperor of France, to establish a Catholic monarchy in the New World. French troops were already in Mexico, and in April 1864, the Austrian Archduke Maximilian, together with his wife, Carlota, accepted the crown of the new empire in what was to be a rather short and tragic reign.

The Eagle stamps first appeared in early May 1864, barely a month before the two young monarchs landed in Mexico at Veracruz. Initially there were, as in the earlier Mexican issues, five denominations: ½r, 1r, 2r, 4r and 8r. In late 1865 a 3-centavo stamp was issued.

Most catalogs list several different overprint types, which are an intriguing feature of the issue. These overprint varieties were really the result of changes in the security system used in the distribution of stamps. The major types correspond to precise periods of use.

Stamps of the First Period, which were issued between May 8 and July 7, 1864, were overprinted with only district names. An example is shown as the left stamp in Figure 5. As noted, these names were applied to Mexican stamps in the offices of the prinicipal districts to which the stamps were sent to validate them for use.

As in the earlier issues, there were instances when the district name was not struck. Such stamps are quite scarce.

By midsummer 1864, the postal administration had devised a refinement to its method of controlling the accounts of stamps sent to the district offices. Each consignment of stamps thereafter was sent from the head office overprinted with an invoice number and the year. When the stamps were received, the district agent was to apply the name of the office to the stamps before their sale and use. For example, the first such shipment went to Guanajuato and carried the numbers "118 1864." An example is shown as the center stamp in Figure 5. Stamps with this additional information (in large numerals) belong to the Second Period, which lasted from July 7 to September 19, 1864.

Then there was a change to a smaller typeface, which gives three more categories: Third Period, balance of 1864; Fourth Period, the entire year of 1865; and Fifth Period, 1866 from January 1 until August 1. The Puebla overprinted stamp shown as the right-hand stamp in

Figure 3. Postally used stamps without district overprints. This pair of 1r stamps has a boxed Huauchinango cancellation. The stamps should have been overprinted either Huejutla or Tulancingo, as both districts supplied stamps to this suboffice.

Figure 4. At top is a stamp of the Tampico district used in Mexico City. At bottom is a stamp of the district of Puebla used at Cordova, a district in the state of Veracruz.

Figure 5 is an example of these small-numeral types. A new stamp issue, showing a profile of Maximilian, was used after that.

To further complicate matters, many of the large principal district offices were responsible for distributing stamps to smaller, suboffices under their jurisdiction. Again, to maintain the accounts, more numbers (usually one or two digits) were added to the stamps before they were dispatched. These suboffice numbers are frequently seen on stamps from Puebla, Queretaro, Guanajuato and San Luis Potosi, all of which had several suboffices. Figure 6 shows a Second Period stamp from Puebla with the number 47 from the suboffice of Tehuacan.

Once in a while, the suboffice name was applied, but not usually. By their nature, suboffices tended to be small towns or haciendas that received few stamps, so examples from these places might be scarce, if not rare.

Stamp shipments to the main office generally contained from several hundred to a few thousand stamps in consignments of the much used denominations (1r and 2r). The lesser used values, ½r, 4r and 8r, were frequently missing from consignments or supplied in very limited quantities.

This business of adding invoice numbers and year dates had the effect of creating virtually thousands of varieties, all of which are eminently collectible.

One should not attempt to tackle this issue without some good reference books at his elbow. Fortunately, there are several good works available. Basic sources include *The Postage Stamps of Mexico 1856-1868* by Samuel Chapman (reprint available); *The Stamps of the Postal Districts of Mexico* by A. Odfjell; and numerous articles that have appeared in *Mexicana*, the journal of the Mexico-Elmhurst Philatelic Society International.

Another book that is particularly helpful when it comes to the suboffice numbers and the towns to which they pertain is *Les Premieres Emissions du Mexique (1856 a 1874)* by Smeth and Fayolle. Although in French, most of the data is readily decipherable.

Armed with one or more of these works, the collector's next

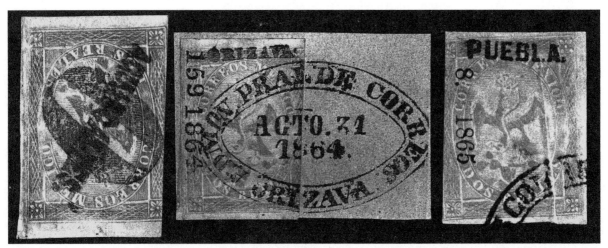

Figure 5. Typical district overprint markings appear on these Eagle stamps. First Period markings (left) show the district name only, in this case Aguascalientes. In the Second Period, invoice numbers were added in large numerals, as shown on this stamp of Orizava (center). The Puebla overprinted stamp (right) shows the small numerals used in the Third, Fourth and Fifth overprinting periods. The stamp also shows a preprinting paper fold.

difficult question might be what to collect and how to organize the collection. As noted previously, there are thousands of varieties, but many of these are very rare, if they exist at all. It is virtually out of the question for one to attempt to form a complete collection, or even one that is nearly complete. However, it is not terribly difficult to assemble a rather comprehensive and interesting type collection of this issue.

One way to start is to secure copies of the five major denominations for each of the five periods. The toughest stamp will be the ½r of the Second Period, Scott 19a. Few exist, and it's seldom offered for sale.

The 3c stamp, Scott 18, only appears in the Fourth and Fifth periods. It is believed to have been an experimental value used on printed matter or drop letters deliverable within Mexico City. A fair number of unused copies have survived. These do appear at auction from time to time, but genuine used copies are exceedingly rare.

A convenient way to expand on the basic types is to develop the collection by districts. The larger districts can account for a great many varieties that are neither scarce nor expensive. Some interesting collecting possibilities also present themselves.

For example, I was able to form a collection of all the consignment number varieties for the principal district office at Orizava. I chose this district because it had no suboffices, it handled a fair amount of mail and, except for two or three cases, received decent-sized shipments of stamps. Even so, it took about 10 years of searching to find all of them.

Another interesting challenge is to find stamps with first-day cancellations on them. It's possible to do this. Tables in the postal archives, which Chapman and others have extracted, show exact dates for most of the consignments.

In the case of Mexico City, it was possible for stamps to have been used the same day the consignments were sent. I have two such examples where a circular datestamp canceler shows the same date as listed for that consignment. One example, a 2r stamp, is shown in Figure 7.

The Eagles issue also provides almost everything else the classic collector likes to study: plate varieties, flaws, colors and shades, and errors in the overprints.

Postal usage is also a wide-open area for study and enjoyment. The late John Bash, who collected and wrote extensively in *Mexicana* about this issue for many years, uncovered much new and interesting information about the Eagle stamps. I highly recommend his articles.

As with the issues of 1856 and 1861, some of these stamps have been manipulated with forged cancellations and overprints. Examples of fractional usage, i.e., bisects, quadrisects, etc., should be checked very carefully. There was a fair quantity of remainders at the end of the issue, so raw material for fabrications was available.

To the timid, I again point out that good reference material exists, and there are experts to help in the difficult situations. Good hunting!

Second issue of the monarchy, 1866-67

Coincident with the regency order authorizing the printing of the Eagle stamps was another decree announcing a decimal-currency system to replace the old peso and reales system (8 reales equaled 1 peso). It's unfortunate the engravers of the Eagles weren't advised of this secret beforehand. It might have saved a lot of confusion. This new decimal system was in effect during most of the time the Eagles were sold, so the rates that worked out to fractional centavos had to be rounded up. For example, ½r equaled 6¼c and was charged at 7c; 1r equaled 12½c and was charged at 13c.

Figure 6. This Second Period stamp of the postal district of Puebla shows the number 47 near the left margin. The number stands for the suboffice of Tehuacan, where this stamp was sold and used.

Figure 7. This 2r stamp from Mexico consignment 25 of 1866 was used the first day it was available, February 1, 1866.

When the city drop rate was tried in 1865, special stamps were printed with the correct decimal rate, 3c. As noted earlier, the 3c stamps were not at all popular and are extremely scarce, especially in used condition.

In June 1866, another decree was issued authorizing and ordering a series of stamps inscribed "Imperio Mexicano" and bearing a portrait of the emperor facing left. The engraving is credited to Senor Gavalon and may have been chosen simply because of the mature look it gave the youthful monarch. We do know there were several other essay designs prepared, many of which show full or three-quarter face views, but these were all discarded for one reason or another.

The new stamps had decimal denominations: 7c, 13c, 25c and 50c. The 3c drop rate for city delivery was abandoned altogether. It's puzzling why there were no peso or 100c values in the series.

The first stamps to appear were lithographed and printed in sheets of 70 subjects on a rather soft paper. Ample supplies were printed and dispatched to the various post offices under French control employing the consignment number and district name overprinting schemes seen on previous issues.

Due to the chaos prevailing at the time, there are many unusual varieties involving mistakes and misinterpretations of postal regulations. The hasty printing resulted in numerous color shades and plate flaws on these stamps.

By this time, Maximilian's forces were losing their grip on remote parts of Mexico, and not all of the shipments of stamps dispatched from Mexico City reached their ultimate destinations. Some were intercepted by liberal forces under Benito Juarez and never saw valid postal use. Further, there are many scarce and rare usages to be found with the Maximilian heads issues.

By mid-October 1866, the postal authorities had succeeded in obtaining engraved stamps of the same design to replace the temporary lithographed series. These stamps were of much better quality but could not be distributed widely because of the ever-shrinking area of influence under Maximilian. For comparison, Figure 8 shows one example each of the lithographed issue and the engraved issue. The engraved stamps circulated during the final months of 1866 and until April of 1867, when the last consignments were issued to Mexico City. An indication of their scarcity is that fewer than a half million stamps were distributed for each series, including all denominations.

The engraved series also provides one of the great classic rarities

Figure 8. These two stamps clearly show the difference in quality between the lithographed stamps (right) and engraved stamps (far right) of the Maximilian issue.

Figure 9. Two values from the engraved remainders. The 25c stamp bears the consignment numbers for Orizava (124 866) but had not been overprinted with the town name to validate it for postal use.

of Mexico. The 7c value, whose primary use would have been for printed circulars, was consigned in very small numbers. Starting in December 1866, only three major cities under royalist control received them: Mexico, Puebla and Veracruz. Only 3,400 stamps were sent out. Of these, 2,000 consigned in a single shipment to Veracruz were lost or destroyed. Of the remaining stamps sent to the other two offices, fewer than a dozen have been found genuinely used. Even unused examples are scarce. A used copy sold at auction several years ago for well in excess of $3,500.

At the close of the issue, sizable quantities of surplus stamps remained for all denominations of the engraved issue, including a large number of the 7c stamps. Many of these overprinted stamps have found their way into the stamp market and may be purchased quite cheaply. Figure 9 shows two values from the engraved remainders. Unfortunately, these remainders have been a nuisance for the classic collector. They have provided an abundant source of raw material for those who create forged overprints and cancellations. Figure 10 shows a pair of the 7c engraved remainders.

Use of the Maximilian stamps ended abruptly in June 1867 when Juarez' forces reoccupied Mexico City. Meanwhile, the unfortunate Maximilian had been captured in Queretaro with his two Mexican generals, Mejia and Miramon, and was sentenced to death by firing squad. Attempts to secure a pardon from Juarez failed, and the execution took place June 19, barely three years after Maximilian had landed in Veracruz with his beautiful young bride.

It was several months before a formal postal system was restored. In the meantime, the resourceful Mexican postal agents resorted to earlier used handstamp methods and limited use of stamps left over from the 1861 issue.

Gothic "Mexico" overprinted stamps

One of the many interesting interludes in Mexican postal affairs during the 19th century are the Gothic name overprints on stamps of Mexico's first design used during 1867-68. These stamps are listed in the *Scott Standard Postage Stamp Catalogue* as 35-45, a group that includes three of the rarest classic stamps of Mexico.

First, some historical perspective is useful. In the spring of 1867, the French-supported monarchy collapsed completely. As previously noted, Archduke Maximilian was executed June 19. The Mexican army occupied the capital on June 21, and President Benito Juarez arrived

Figure 10. A pair of 7c Maximilian engraved remainders. This denomination has been tampered with extensively with counterfeit names and consignment numbers added to deceive stamp collectors.

Figure 11. An example of the stamped impression of the 1867-68 "Mexico" overprint. The style of lettering gives the Gothic overprinted issues their name.

in the city on July 15.

On August 6, a decree was issued to the secretary of the treasury for reorganization of fiscal matters, including the collection and distribution of revenue.

New postage stamps would be designed and printed, but these would not appear until September 1868. Continued use of stamps of the deposed monarch was unthinkable. Meanwhile, postal authorities located remainders of the 1861 issue, mostly 1r and 2r stamps.

Because the relatively small quantities were insufficient to service the entire country, it was determined that these remainders would be reissued for local use only. The rest of the post offices in the republic would revert to the sello negro handstamp system for franking letters. Sello negro literally translates "black (hand)stamp." It refers to the pre-stamp franking practice.

The first of Mexico's first-issue remainder stamps appear to have been issued and used without a name overprint. We might speculate that postal clerks, aware that the stamps were intended for use only in the Mexico district, considered the overprinting unnecessary. Numerous covers bearing unoverprinted stamps with June and July 1867 dates have been recorded.

At about the same time, an order was given to clean up the plates of the 1861 issue and reprint the four low denominations, excluding the 8r value. This order gave rise to the 1867 reissue (Scott 42-45) printed on thin gray revenue paper with large "R.P.S." (Renta Papel Sellado) watermark. The watermark appeared about three times in each sheet of stamps, so about half of the reissued stamps will show parts of it. It was not a large printing. Only 15,000 ½r stamps, 26,200 1r stamps, 81,320 2r stamps and 13,470 4r stamps came off the presses. Postal records indicate that most, if not all, of these thin-paper stamps were sold. Unused examples, particularly the 1r and 4r denominations, are scarce and high-priced, suggesting that the majority were used on mail.

Name overprinting, the normal Mexican post office practice to validate stamps for use, seems to have resumed in earnest at about the time the thin-paper stamps were issued, and continued until the full-face Hidalgos came into use 13 months later.

Figure 11 shows the stamped impression of the "Mexico" name in Gothic letters, applied with the same device used for overprinting the

Figure 12. Two 2r stamps with the Gothic Mexico overprint: a printing on pinkish paper from the 1861 remainders (right) and a printing in green on thin paper of the 1867 reissue (far right). Typical of the remainders, the overprint is extremely difficult to see on the stamp at right.

8

Eagle and Maximilian issues. The earliest recorded use of the Gothic "Mexico" overprint is August 9.

Collecting these Gothic overprints can be frustrating for the fussy collector. Much of the 1861 remainder stock, especially the 1r and 2r stamps, had been poorly printed, and clear impressions are hard to find. The thin-paper reissues generally get better marks in this respect.

Figure 12 shows the difference in printing quality between these issues. The vertical "Mexico" overprint is barely visible on the 2r remainder issue on the left, beginning at the "OS" of "DOS" on the stamp's design and running upward. It is easily seen on the 1867 reissue on the right.

Further, the name overprints and cancellations are often found smudged, reflecting carelessness on the part of the postal workers. Since use was limited to Mexico, the usual cancellations were double-ring datestamp types common to the period.

These Gothic overprinted stamps are the source of a fair number of varieties with the overprint printed on both sides, especially among the 1861 1r and 2r remainders. These are not common, to be sure, but are relatively more plentiful than similar varieties on the regular issues of 1856 and 1861. This is another indication that the remainder stock was of substandard quality to begin with.

While the vast majority of Gothic overprinted stamps are found with Mexico City cancellations or on covers originating there, an occasional letter crops up from a nearby town. Figure 13 shows a cover

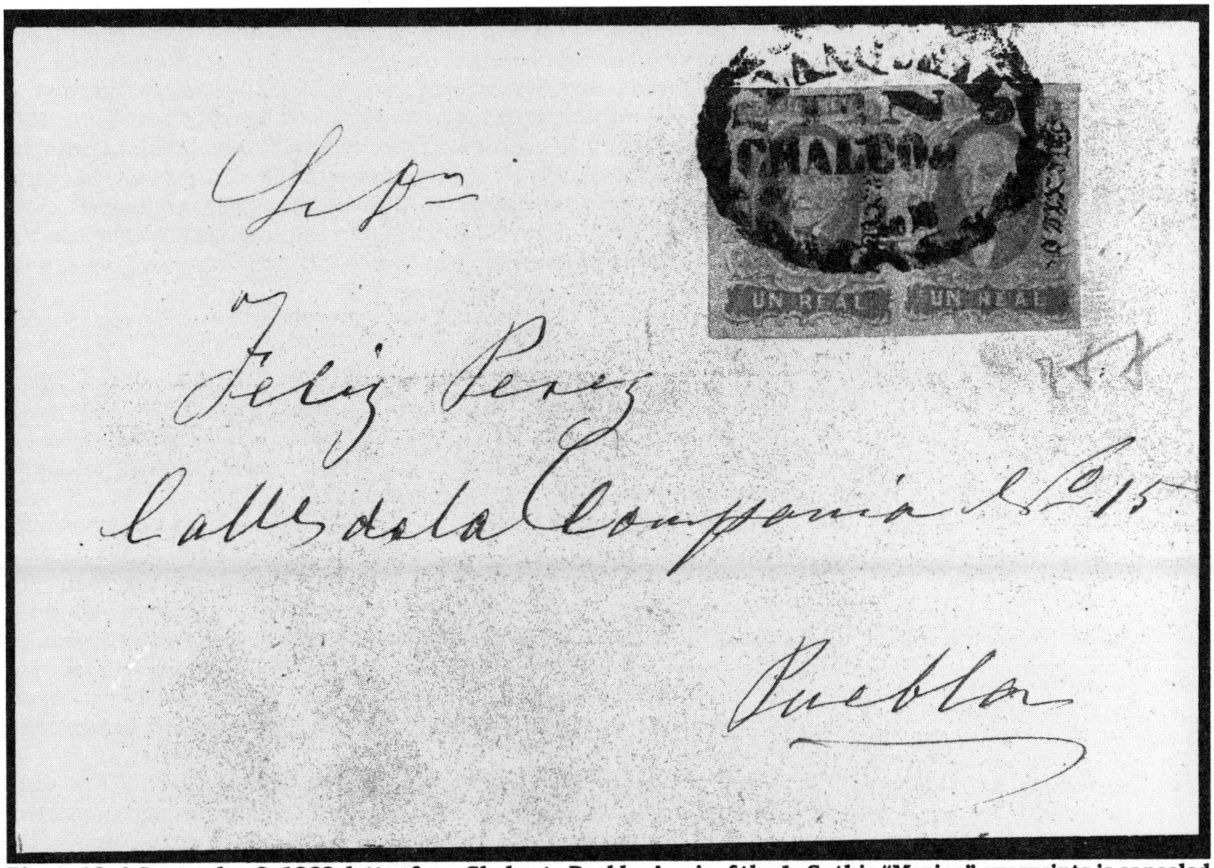

Figure 13. A September 9, 1868, letter from Chalco to Puebla. A pair of the 1r Gothic "Mexico" overprints is canceled with an oval wreath "Franqueado/EN/Chalco" handstamp.

from my collection bearing a pair of the 1r Gothics mailed from and canceled in Chalco, a small village southeast of Mexico City. It is dated September 9, 1868, at the very end of the usage period. In fact, the full-face Hidalgo stamps were already on sale in Mexico City. At this time, all but the 1r Gothic overprinted stamps had been sold out.

The scarcest of these Gothic overprinted stamps, and the key stamps in any collection of the first-design varieties, are the ½r black-on-buff, the 4r on white paper, and the 8r green-on-brown. There was no record of these denominations in the remainders inventory of May 1864, when use of the Eagle stamps became mandatory.

It is generally assumed that the ½r stamps were probably among returns from outlying post offices received later. The rare 8r stamps may have been partial sheets mixed in with the returned 8r black-on-brown stamps. In any event, so limited were their numbers that no separate record of them was kept.

The 4r on white paper is a special case. Some experts believe that these stamps were made when a new printing of 4r stamps on normal paper was ordered in the summer of 1867. The Scott catalog formerly priced this stamp, but discontinued the listing in the early 1980s. So many of the stamps purporting to be this variety turn out to be 1856 remainders with forged overprints that genuine copies rarely appear on the market.

Over the years, some students of Mexican philately have refused to accept the Gothic overprints as regular issues. They claim, with a certain logic, that these stamps were strictly limited in their use and should be classified as provisionals.

In this same period, the district of Guadalajara issued an extensive series of provisional stamps. The state of Chiapas and the town of Cuernavaca did too, but authentically used copies are rare.

As you would expect, the forgers have been at work with the Gothic overprints, especially the rare values. Many are rather crudely done and not too difficult to distinguish. A few cheap 2r Eagles with clear name overprints can serve as good examples for comparison to detect the more obvious fakes. Still, the valuable Gothic overprinted stamps should always be acquired with extreme care, as many dangerous forged overprints do exist.

Full-face Hidalgos of 1868-72

In many respects, the issue of 1868-72 offers almost everything a specialist could want. These are the stamps that the Scott catalog lists between numbers 46 and 80. Most Mexican specialists refer to them as the full-face Hidalgos. Miguel Hidalgo, pictured on the stamps, was the father of Mexican independence.

The stamps came out after a period of about a year when postage stamps were unavailable and postal authorities had to revert to pre-stamp franking practices. This situation was forced by the sudden end of the Maximilian affair. There was insufficient time to design and produce a suitable stamp for the restored Republican government.

As noted, some old stocks of the first design were used in Mexico City (validated by a name overprint in Gothic characters), but the rest of the country went without stamps from about July 1867 to September 1868.

Some collectors claim the full-face Hidalgos are Mexico's ugliest stamps. That may be true, but in this case, appearance has not discouraged interest in their philatelic charms. They were a favorite of many early Mexico specialists and are enjoying a revival in popularity.

The Scott catalog divides them into two main groups: stamps

with thin figures of value and those with thick figures. Some of these issues received "Anotado" overprints, which will be discussed later.

Within the main groups are listed imperforate stamps and perforated stamps. Actually, there are several perforation varieties because of experiments with stamp separation at the printing office. The Scott catalog lists of subvarieties call attention to a few of the notable printing mistakes, flaws and paper varieties, but these barely scratch the surface of what's available if you enjoy this sort of thing. Shown in Figure 14 is a subvariety of the 50c stamp. There is no period after the "50" in the denomination label. The overprint shows the district name "Veracruz," the consignment number "2" (over the "O" in "MEXICO") and the year "71" (just above the "T" in "CENT").

As with preceding issues, the system of district name overprinting and consignment numbers gives an opportunity to form a specialized collection. There were 41 numbers with abbreviated year dates and 43 district names. Stamps from some of the smaller districts are difficult to locate, and many are rare. Also, the high values — 50c and 100c — are, as expected, somewhat pricey, especially the brown-on-brown 100c stamps with thin figures.

An array of lithographic transfer types and retouches attracts serious collectors to this issue. This was only the second Mexican issue to be produced by lithography. (The Maximilian profile stamps were the first.) Printers were still learning how best to prepare their stones (plates) for large quantities of stamps. This led to numerous varieties.

There are 10 transfer types for each of the five denominations. These occurred when the lithographic transports were made to form the plates. The types have been studied and written about extensively, so it is not difficult to categorize them. It's a simple matter of flyspeck philately: careful examination of hundreds of stamps under moderate magnification. A booklet by Roberto Garcia-Larranaga and published by MEPSI will steer you through this maze. The illustration in Figure 15 is taken from this booklet. It shows the locations of plate flaws and retouches on this issue.

The area of retouches is a vast field for study. Retouches were attempts to correct minor flaws in the design. These flaws occurred during the transfer process. Because of the large number of stones needed and the number of transfer operations for each stone, retouches became quite numerous.

Swedish collector Gunnar Benson spent many years working on these stamps. He and John Heath, another student of this issue, were working on a handbook at the time of Benson's death in 1987. It is hoped Heath can complete this work, as it would be a welcome addition to the reference libraries of serious collectors of Mexico.

The major portion of Benson's studies deals with the 25c thick-figure stamp and the seven stones used in its printing. Since 25c was then the most common rate, these stamps are plentiful and not terribly expensive. However, one needs a large number of them to get started on any serious plating studies and so should look for job lots or a specialized collection with which to begin. These should not be too difficult to find. I have noticed some in recent auctions of Mexican material. Remainder collections are another source, since a dealer usually will not take the time to sort through the collection for scarce types or retouches. He usually is content with picking out the more desirable Scott-listed items.

There is a fair amount of literature on the 1868 Hidalgos. Overprinted consignment number varieties are well covered in *Catalogo Especializado de los Sellos Postales de Mexico* by Eduardo Aguirre. This

Figure 14. This 50c stamp is a subvariety listed by Scott as 62a. There is no period after the "50" in the denomination label. The overprint shows the district name "Veracruz," the consignment number "2" (over the "O" in "MEXICO") and the year "71" (just above the "T" in "CENT").

Figure 15. This graphic was developed by Roberto Garcia-Larranaga to describe locations of plate flaws and retouches on the 1868-72 full-face Hidalgo issue of Mexico.

also shows the relative scarcity of district varieties.

If one is intent on pursuing the types and retouches in depth, I first recommend the specialized study by Garcia-Larranaga. One should also obtain Benson's articles, numbering about 14, which have appeared from time to time between January 1982 and January 1987 in *Mexicana*, the journal of MEPSI.

A comprehensive listing of older literature relating to the 1868-72 Hidalgo issue can be found in volume 17, number 3 of the *Philatelic Literature Review* published by the American Philatelic Research Library. Most, if not all, of these references are available to American Philatelic Society members at the library.

Counterfeit "Anotado" overprints

In the spring of 1872 it was announced that there would be a new issue of stamps to replace those that had been in service since 1868. Several interesting theories have been offered to explain this sudden change after barely four years of use.

One popular suggestion was that functionaries within the postal agency were syphoning off supplies of stamps and manipulating them (by applying counterfeit overprints and consignment numbers) and selling them to large commercial users for personal gain. That's possible, but as yet it's an unproven theory.

The 1868 issue showed a full-face portrait of Father Miguel Hidalgo y Costilla. The new design showed him in profile facing left. The new issue was to be placed on sale March 1, 1872 (or perhaps somewhat later; it is not known for certain). Also, the postal administration in Mexico City had already begun to recall surplus stamps of the old issue from outlying postal districts.

For some reason, the new stamps were not ready by March 1. Since many of the old ones had been demonetized and removed from

Anotado

Figure 16. An approximate facsimile of the "Anotado" overprint.

the official accounts, it was feared that a severe shortage of stamps would arise. Authorities decided to overprint some of the surplus stamps that had been returned. The overprint read "Anotado" (which means noted or accounted for). Thus the stamps were validated for temporary use until the new stamps were delivered. An approximate facsimile of the overprint is shown in Figure 16. Properly overprinted stamps are shown in Figure 17.

The overprinted "Anotado" stamps were intended for use only at the Principal Postal Administration in Mexico City. None was sent to other district offices in the interior. These district offices were to use whatever stocks of stamps they had remaining or to revert to the sello negro (handstamp) system of indicating postage paid. For this reason, it may seem unusual to see postmarks of districts other than Mexico on the overprinted stamps, but they are often found among the few of these stamps that do survive.

As noted, all of this occurred in a short span of time during the spring of 1872. Since no one has yet found official records concerning this "Anotado" usage, the period of legitimate use had to be established from dated covers or letters bearing the stamps.

Fortunately a large business correspondence was found in Guanajuato. This correspondence contained a fair number of letters bearing the "Anotado" stamps. Since the sequence in the correspondence contained letters from nearly every day during the period, it was possible to deduce the time of use fairly precisely. The first date found was March 12; the last date was April 25.

What we can conclude is that there was a period of only about 40 days during which the "Anotado" stamps were used. Naturally, the net result is stamps and covers of considerable scarcity. They are listed in all the major catalogs.

The new 1872 issue finally made its appearance in the early days of April 1872.

Unfortunately, there are many fake "Anotado" overprints. Warnings to this effect are given in all catalogs and should be heeded. Some of these fake overprints have been so poorly executed that even an untrained eye can detect them.

Collectors should also note that many of the genuine overprints were not well struck, so an incomplete or smudgy overprint does not automatically relegate it to the bad category.

A few quick tests will eliminate many stamps and covers from the ranks of the genuine. If one has a full, dated cover — and many purists will collect these stamps in no other way — it should fall into the time span noted: March 12 to April 25. This does not mean there can't be a genuine cover outside this range, but it's bound to be a long shot.

Figure 17. This strip of three 12c stamps returned from the Lagos district was validated for use with "Anotado" overprints.

Figure 18. A 25c "Anotado" stamp with Gothic-type district overprint of Mexico (1-72) franked this cover from Mexico City to Veracruz dated March 22, 1872.

The cover shown in Figure 18 has a faint business datestamp on its face with "March/22/1872" inside a blue oval. The cover also is docketed March 22, so it falls in the middle of the accepted period of use. The cover in Figure 19, bearing a pair of the 12c stamps, is dated April 9, nearer the end of the estimated period of use. Both covers are unquestionably genuine.

The other test is whether a used stamp bears a contemporary cancellation of Mexico City. This will invariably be a double-ring circular datestamp. Most good examples I have seen were not particu-

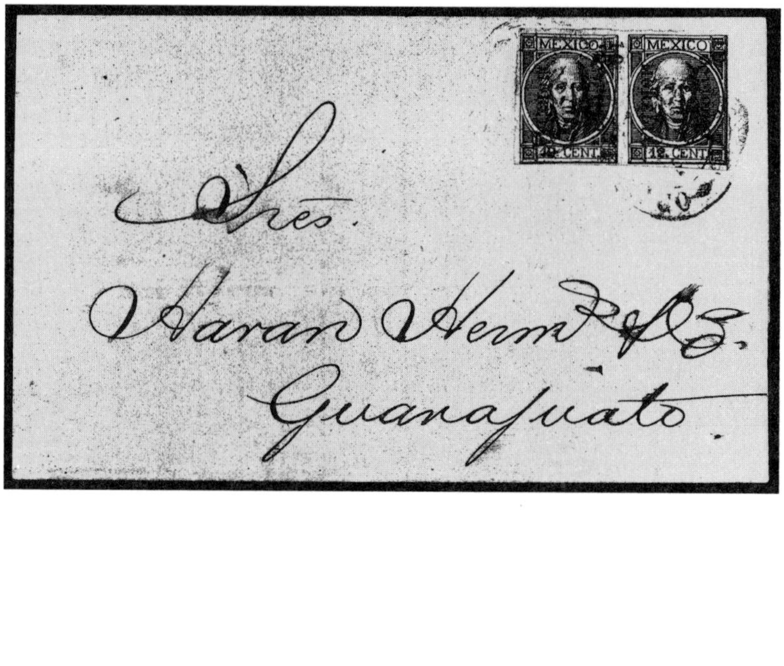

Figure 19. A pair of 12c stamps returned from the Morelia district (10-71) were used on this letter dated April 9, 1872, from Mexico City to Guanajuato.

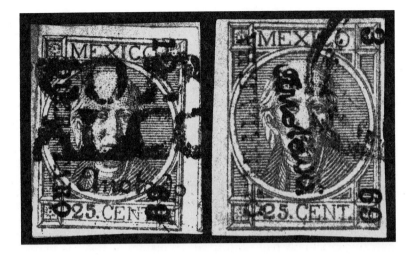

Figure 20. These two stamps have forged "Anotado" overprints and bear cancellations from suboffices in the Queretaro and Guadalajara districts, even though the overprint was authorized only for use at the Mexico City post office.

larly well struck. From the standpoint of beauty's sake, this is unfortunate, but there is a bright side to the matter. Many of the forgers apparently decided their illegitimate cancellations should at least look attractive. These forged cancellations are usually more clearly applied than the real ones. Beware of neat cancellations.

The stamps with forged cancellations illustrated in Figure 20 bear postmarks of offices other than Mexico and are easily distinguished. In these instances, the perpetrator obviously ignored the fact that the stamps were authorized for use only at the Mexico City office.

If you find one of these overprinted stamps and contemplate purchasing it, you would be well advised to buy it only on the condition that it receives a good certificate of authenticity. Spurn like the plague any offers of "as yet unrecorded Anotado in blue, violet or reddish purple." The genuine overprints are always black.

Clues for detecting forged stamps and overprints

Manufacturing rare stamps to deceive collectors seems to have been a popular, if not profitable, business since the stamp hobby began. Collectors and dealers often tell me they shy away from the classic stamps of Mexico because the stamps are, as they put it, so difficult and there are so many fakes, forgeries and counterfeits.

The same statement can be made for many other countries and other classic issues. But I suspect the person responding this way may not have the desire, time or drive to educate himself so he can avoid being taken in and, more importantly, so he will be able to distinguish between the good items and bad items.

By relating some history about forgeries of classic Mexican stamps, especially the first issues, I hope to help collectors feel more comfortable about collecting Mexican classics.

In his book, *Album Weeds*, the Reverend Robert Earee describes seven different forgeries of the Mexican first issue (1856). Most of the forgeries he describes, however, were so poorly and crudely produced that there is no reason the observant collector who is familiar with the first design should be fooled.

But there have been two great waves of forgery activity that have proved to be much more troublesome. The first took place about 1895-1910; the second coincided with World War II and the two decades following. Figure 21 shows a strip from a turn-of-the-century French stamp album. Only the 2r stamp at the center is genuine.

About 1893, a man from St. Louis offered a well-known and

respected British stamp firm at least three plates prepared for printing the 1r and 2r first-design stamps of Mexico (1856-68). How he gained possession of these plates was never revealed, but it is virtually certain they were taken from the Postal Museum in Mexico City.

In any event, the offer was rejected. As it turned out, plates for the other denominations also had been removed along with remainder stocks of the official colored papers used for the 1861 issue. With this material, two essential ingredients were available for the forging of postage stamps. We now know what happened.

The plates were used chiefly to reprint the scarce 4r and 8r denominations of the 1856 and 1861 series, although many ½r stamps of the 1861 type also were made. The stamps are Scott 4-6 and 9-12. These are the same reprints referred to in the italicized notes at the end of the first two catalog listings. Forgeries of the 1856 issue are shown in Figure 22.

The forgers obviously had extensive knowledge of the stamps and how they originally had been used. To further complicate matters, reprinted stamps were doctored with district name overprints and cancellations to make them appear authentic. In some instances, the forgers were able to use some of the original canceling devices that had also been purloined from the Postal Museum.

These fabrications were eased into the stamp market. From the number of examples that have been definitely identified, it seems they received eager acceptance from collectors all over the world. However, some astute collectors and dealers from Great Britain and continental Europe began to recognize these as forgeries. Articles started to appear in the philatelic press in the 1910s and early 1920s.

Probably the best summary of information was released in 1935 in the previously mentioned book, *Les Premieres Emissions du Mexique (1856-1874),* by the French team of Paul de Smeth and Marquis de Fayolle. The section on forgeries was translated and published by MEPSI in early issues of *Mexicana.* These experts, aided by many others, have unlocked most of the secrets used by the reprinters so that we have a basis for distinguishing the reprints from the originals.

Some of the differences are not very profound. Even though original plates and paper were used in the printing, the experts recognized that nearly all of the reprints of the 1861 stamps have the grain of the wove paper running in the wrong direction. It is vertical

Figure 21. In this strip, snipped from a turn-of-the-century French stamp album, only the 2r stamp at the center is genuine. The other four are crude forgeries.

Figure 22. Forgeries of the 1856 issue: The 4r stamp carries the district name of Ometepec, which never existed as a postal district. Were it genuine, the 8r stamp from Acapulco would be a great rarity. But it shows all the standard fake characteristics: poor color, thick paper and a stop (period) at the foot of the final "O" in the forged name overprint.

instead of horizontal. Thus, the simple test of holding a suspect stamp to the light often suffices to identify bad stamps. Examples of these papers are shown in Figure 23. Forgeries of the 1861 issue are shown in Figure 24. I caution collectors that horizontal grain is not an absolute check of authenticity. A few reprints are known with the grain running in the proper direction.

Only reprints of the 4r and 8r were made of the 1856 issue. There were plenty of genuine ½r stamps around, and they were cheap. The reprinted 1856 stamps were on a very thick, very white paper that is fairly easy to distinguish when compared side by side with an original.

Another clue is the ink. The red colors of the 4r reprints are usually dull and less vivid than the genuine stamps. Similarly, the inks used to print the 8r forgeries tend to be grayer and often have a muddy appearance. The colors are distinctively different from the clear lilac and lilac-purple shades of the genuine stamps.

Another tip is the impressions. The reprints were mostly produced from plates showing advanced wear and often exhibiting crude attempts at recutting weak lines.

The overprinting with district names and cancellations was so cleverly done in many instances that knowledgeable collectors and dealers were deceived at first. Part of the problem was that there weren't many references or accurate reproductions of the postal markings available at that time. This information had to be developed from reliable sources, such as full, dated letters, and then communicated to the collecting community.

W.T. Wilson's book, *The Postmarks of Mexico, 1856-1872* (1927), gave collectors something to use in checking cancellations. The Smeth-Fayolle book gave detailed characteristics of the fake district-name overprints.

These brief paragraphs cannot transform you into an instant expert on high-value 1856-61 Hidalgo heads. There are many other factors to be considered, and the process of rendering an expert opinion is often long and arduous. But I hope you will exercise wariness when such items are offered to you for sale.

To summarize, there are several things to keep in mind. The 1r and 2r values of both issues and the ½r of 1856 were so common that few forgeries were made. In fact, some specialists are willing to pay more for these forgeries than they would for the genuine stamps (of

Figure 23. Back-lit enlargements from 1861 stamps show the vertical paper grain found only on forgeries (top) and horizontal grain found on all genuine stamps and some forgeries (bottom).

Figure 24. Forgeries of the 1861 issue: Both stamps are easily classified as forgeries by the vertical grain test. The 4r stamp also shows the worn-plate impression and a district name that is too small. The cancellation would be difficult to condemn. The 8r forgery has similar shortcomings but again has reasonably authentic-looking postal markings.

common districts). A 4r or 8r stamp should be examined closely. Those that arouse suspicion should be examined by experts. This is particularly true for the scarce districts.

Most reputable dealers now take the precaution of obtaining certification prior to sale. Also, most of the rare items in this category carry with them an established pedigree. That's often a big advantage.

Hidalgo Profile issue of 1872-74

For some collectors, the Hidalgo Profiles represent the nadir of Mexican stamp design. These stamps rarely have been shown in exhibitions. The eminent British stamp collector J.H. Barron described these stamps in the May 1915 issue of the *Philatelic Journal of Great Britain* as follows:

"Faultily drawn, the portrait of Miguel Hidalgo stands up uncertainly from a muddy background surrounded by a miscellany of conventional ornaments which are crowded into every available space."

Figure 25 shows the 100c high value of the issue. True, this stamp and the others of the issue are certainly not beauties, but they do have charms for the collector. Considering the circumstances under which they were issued, we may understand and forgive the Mexican postal authorities for this hastily produced set.

The previous issue, which showed a full-face portrait of Hidalgo, had fallen into disrepute because of a postal fraud wherein post office employees sold counterfeit stamps to enrich themselves. Top postal officials wanted a new set of stamps as quickly as possible, with safeguards against a recurrence of the private printings by postal workers. A postal directive specified the month of April 1872 for the changeover from the old stamps to the Hidalgo Profiles, but it is clear that the two issues were in use simultaneously during May and probably early June.

The designer of the Hidalgo Profile stamps is unknown. He was probably an employee of the government printing office. It is believed that one master die with blank panels was made from which were produced five copper cliches for the various denominations. Each of the five denominations shows some differences in the printing of all the wording. On the 6c stamp, the word "SEIS" appears in the left panel, although on all others the inscribed denomination is in the right panel.

Lithographic transfers were taken from the five cliches to make

Figure 25. The 100c high value of the 1872 Hidalgo Profile issue.

up the stones that printed each sheet of stamps. The final layout pattern was a 100-stamp sheet printed 10 by 10, although there is evidence that at one point in production there were sheets with only 90 subjects. Transfer types have been identified, as well as numerous retouches and other plate flaws. This area can give hours of enjoyment to the collector who loves to look at stamps through a strong magnifying glass. Plating studies of most of the lower denominations have been completely reconstructed. Those of the high values have not been, so far as I know, because of the cost and difficulty of obtaining multiples.

There seems to have been considerable difficulty in procuring adequate stocks of white paper needed for this issue. The stamps display an astonishing variety of paper thicknesses ranging from very thick to extremely thin.

Even fiscal paper was used for printing the stamps, which gave rise to the "PAPEL SELLADO" watermarked varieties. The top of Figure 26 shows this large watermark. It appeared only once or possibly twice on a single sheet of stamps, so stamps that show it are relatively scarce.

Figure 26 also shows a watermark with "LA F" in large double-line block letters and a heraldic cross and a hyphen between the "A" and the "F." This watermark is a rebus for LaCroix Freres, a French papermaking firm. It is often seen on lettersheets of the period. Its presence on Mexican postal and revenue issues of 1872 suggests that postal authorities may have purchased ordinary writing paper in order to print stamps.

Stamp separation was another problem. There were numerous schemes being tested at the time, most of which were not too successful. The Mexico City district was supplied regularly with perforated stamps, but the outlying district offices usually received imperforate stocks.

As Figure 27 shows, perforations of various shapes and sizes were tried, most between gauges 13 and 15 as seen on the stamp on the left. Pinhole perforations, as seen on the right-hand stamp, proved largely ineffective. Most stamps with them were cut apart when used.

Consignment numbers and district name overprints offer an interesting and challenging field of specialization. There were 51 different consignment numbers used on the Hidalgo Profiles, one for each district office. Mexico City was number 1, for example, and Zacatecas was number 51. Although these stamps were in service for little more than two years, three different year dates are found in conjunction with the consignment numbers: (18)72, 73 and 74.

A few numbering errors are known, and there was at least one reported case in which shipments to two districts, Morelia and Orizava, were switched. Since the stamps were used anyway, they appear to carry the wrong invoice number.

Figure 26. Parts of these large watermarks are sometimes found on Hidalgo Profiles. The revenue-paper watermark is shown at top left, and the papermaker's watermark is shown at bottom left.

Figure 27. Perforated 1872 issues most commonly originated in Mexico City, including this 6c (right), crudely perforated in gauge 13, and a pin-perforated 50c Hidalgo Profile (far right).

The smaller post offices received and sold few copies of these relatively short-lived issues. Examples from some post offices can be quite difficult to find.

The issue also includes an interesting color error to tantalize collectors. It seems that the 50c denomination was printed in blue, the correct color of the 12c stamp. Although most of these errors were found before they got into circulation, a few sheets slipped into the distribution system. Some of these were legitimately used.

For all the criticism the 1872 Hidalgo Profiles received, they did have one advantage over the issue they replaced. On the back of each stamp was a security-printing device, a blue pattern of rippled lines referred to as moire (pronounced mwa-RAY). Figure 28 shows the design as it appears on the back of the 6c stamp in Figure 27.

While the moire pattern may have helped prevent postal forgeries, it curiously failed to deter those who forged stamps for sale to collectors. The best known of these counterfeits are those produced by the Spiro brothers of Hamburg, Germany. Ironically, the Spiro forgeries show much better craftsmanship than the authentic issues, although they differ in minor details. Also, the moire pattern, though closely matching the genuine stamps, appears too bold and too blue.

Unfortunately, there are still many examples of the Spiro fakes in circulation, particularly in older collections, since they were widely marketed and actually looked better than the genuine article.

For reference material on the Hidalgo Profile issue, I recommend a series of articles by Franco Vanotti that appeared in *Mexicana* between 1984 and 1986. In Vanotti's treatment, the work of Barron and other specialists of this issue has been added to, updated and corrected. These articles would be especially useful for plating studies.

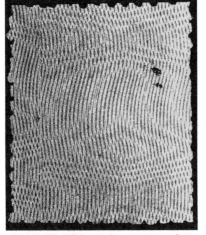

Figure 28. This moire pattern, from the back of the 6c stamp from Figure 27, was a security device intended to deter forgers.

Chapter 2

The Porfirian Era, 1877-1910

Control codes on Hidalgo heads

For nearly 30 years following the introduction of stamps in Mexico in 1856, portraits of Father Miguel Hidalgo y Costilla were the invariable motif of Mexican stamps. The only exceptions were during the monarchy (1864-67), when the Mexican imperial eagle and Archduke Maximilian were the subjects of stamp design.

The two lithographed issues immediately following the monarchy period weren't especially attractive, although numerous varieties make them good material for the serious specialist. These issues certainly did not compare favorably with contemporary stamps of other countries from the standpoint of design and workmanship.

This probably inspired the Mexican postal authorities to release a more attractive issue. The Hidalgo head issue of 1874-83 went on sale May 5, 1874, the seventh anniversary of the Mexican victory over the French in the Battle of Puebla.

Mexico was struggling for a new, more modern identity. Postal authorities had the 1874 issue designed, engraved and printed by the American Bank Note Company of New York, and the stamps represented high-quality production. There were five denominations, from 5c to 100c, all showing Hidalgo's profile facing left.

Figure 29. These two stamps show the normal wide-number format used for overprinting until 1877.

Figure 30. After 1878, the control numbers were printed with the district number (in this case, 53) close to the year (78).

Like their predecessors, these stamps underwent an elaborate control treatment with overprints to forestall unauthorized use in the event of theft or misappropriation. But this issue and a companion series, the Juarez stamps (1879-82), issued exclusively for foreign mail, were among the last ones to suffer this cumbersome process. The system involved imprinting control numbers and year dates on the stamps before shipment to the outlying district offices. Once the stamps were received there, local postal authorities were supposed to add district name overprints before selling them.

This overprinting on the early issues of Mexico generated countless varieties. Collectors can't seem to resist the temptation to search for as many as they can find. In this instance there are plenty of different names and numbers to look for.

From 1874 to 1877, the dispatch overprint, consisting of a control number (a different one for each district) and the last two digits of the year date, was applied near the middle of the stamp. These have become known as the wide-apart, or separated, numbers (Figure 29).

There was a system for the control numbers, too. Mexico City was assigned control number 1, and successive numbers were assigned to the rest of the districts in alphabetical order: 2 to Acapulco, 3 to Aguascalientes, and so forth. There is a complication to this. After 51 was assigned to Zacatecas, which is at the end of the usual list of districts, several more districts were added. These districts were assigned control numbers 52 through 61. Many of the added names had been suboffices in earlier times, although for some reason, Guanajuato, which was a large principal office, was skipped in the normal sequence and given number 52.

Commencing in 1878, the control number and the last two digits of the year were printed together, resulting in the so-called close-number varieties (Figure 30). Furthermore, the alphabetical listing order was reversed. Thus, in 1878 the numeric designation for Zamora was 178, Zacatecas was 278, Veracruz was 378, and so forth. Mexico City, the largest district, was given the control number 5478. Colima must have come as an afterthought and was assigned 5578.

Normally, the unseparated numbers were placed near the top or upper right corner of the stamps. However, for a short period in 1878 some were imprinted near the bottom (Figure 31). These are considerably scarcer, and such stamps from some districts are unquestionably

Figure 31. The control numbers are placed at the bottom of these two stamps.

rare. Experts feel this probably happened on only one shipment, perhaps the first. This would explain their scarcity.

Other changes occurred. In 1878 the color of the 10c stamp was switched from black to orange. And, to cover a change in postal rates, a 4c in orange was added to the series in 1880. These are noted in the Scott catalog listings.

Near the end of 1877, American Bank Note Company transferred the printing plates to the Mexican government printing office. The stamps were henceforth produced in Mexico. This transfer coincided with the appearance of the numerous paper and watermark varieties, since the Mexicans apparently used paper from various sources.

These varieties include the so-called horizontally laid paper, the "LA + F" (La Croix Freres, a French papermaker) watermarked paper, and the "PAPEL SELLADO" (Mexican) watermarked paper. Both watermarks are shown as Figure 26 on page 19.

In the final two years of the issue, virtually all stamps were printed on a distinctive thin, unwatermarked wove paper.

All these combinations created hundreds of collectible varieties. Figure 32 shows a stamp with the control number inverted.

As in the earlier issues, the two high values, 50c and 100c, are scarce since few were needed for normal mail. The smaller offices often received none, or at most received only a few hundred copies. Some years no stamps were sent because inventory stocks were adequate.

Common denominations are likewise scarce to rare for post offices like Texcoco, Tacubaya, Huejutla, Soyaniquilpan and Cuautitlan. These same offices are the difficult ones to find on the preceding issues as well. Small towns like these didn't generate much mail. In fact, five small districts (Guadalupe Hidalgo, Otumba, Tepeji del Rio, Tlalnepantla and Tlalpam), which received stamps directly in the initial 1874 distribution, were dropped from the list because of low sales. Only a few stamps have ever been found from these towns. These stamps can be considered great rarities.

For would-be specialists, there are a few reference works on this issue. Bruce L. Chittenden published a monograph (*Collectors' Club Handbook* number 1) in 1918 that deals extensively with the papers and watermarks. Calvert Steir wrote articles in 1950 for the *Collector's Club Philatelist* that simplify and clarify the Chittenden work.

Probably the best source of information on the varieties that exist is a book by R.R. Billings titled *Mexico — Postal Issue of 1874-1883*. I believe Billings published it himself privately in 1960, and it may be difficult to locate. The American Philatelic Research Library should have a copy.

From various sources, including some of the Mexican official postal records, Billings tabulated all the various stamps known to have been issued and the total shipments to (and returns from) the district offices. He also included data on the scarce to rare stamps he was able to locate in important collections around the world. Unfortunately, some postal records were not complete, so estimates had to be made. But the Billings data does give a good basis to judge whether a given number and overprint name is run-of-the-mill or something special.

Until a few years ago, this group of Hidalgo heads was not as popular as the engraved stamps issued prior to 1867. However, they have received more attention lately, probably because they are still less expensive than the earlier classics and offer a similar collecting challenge. Another advantage is that, to my knowledge, there have been no reprints or forgeries that might scare some collectors.

The aspect of postal history shouldn't be overlooked. As noted,

Figure 32. Note that the control number on this stamp has been applied inverted.

Figure 33. This unoverprinted 25c Juarez stamp from the 1879 thick-paper printing has a plate crack at the top left.

the Hidalgo heads represent the last major issue to receive number and name overprints, which track usage, routing and so forth. The stamps also were used on foreign mail until the Juarez stamps were issued in 1879. Thereafter the use of the Hidalgo heads was confined to domestic mail. Foreign usages generally required more than one stamp, and some eye-appealing combinations exist.

To me, the bottom line on this issue is that it offers a broad scope for serious philatelic study equally as interesting as the earlier classic stamps with one important difference—it can be done at less than half the price of the earlier classics.

Juarez issues of 1879-83

One of the quirks in the history of Mexican postal affairs is that for a period of about four years, there were two distinct stamp issues in simultaneous use.

The Hidalgo issue was used to frank both domestic and foreign mail until 1879, when Mexico joined the Universal Postal Union.

After Mexico gained UPU membership, another set of stamps, called the Juarez issue (Scott 123-45), was prepared. It was so named because the stamps bore the portrait of Benito Juarez, hero of the War of Reform and president of the Mexican Republic during and after the period of French occupation, from 1863 to 1867. These stamps were for exclusive use on foreign-bound mail, while the Hidalgo stamps were reserved for use on domestic mail.

The reason for this dual system was quite simple. One of the objectives of the UPU was to standardize mail rates among the member countries. At that time, a half-ounce foreign letter was to be charged at 25 French centimes or 5¢ in U.S. currency. Since the peso was almost at par with the U.S. dollar, Mexico wanted to adhere to a 5-centavo rate. However, Mexico's internal postal rates were extremely high. For example, a domestic letter weighing one-half ounce was charged 25c up to 45 miles and 35c beyond that distance.

The idea of separate issues for foreign and for internal use was a neat solution to this problem. The stamps would clearly signal to postal workers that letters were foreign-bound. They also would facilitate sorting and accounting.

There were eight values in the first Juarez series, from 1c to 100c, cataloged as Scott 123-30. These were printed on fairly thick wove

Figure 34. The 2c and 3c denominations of the Small Numerals series of 1882-83. These Small Numeral stamps belong to the foreign-mail series.

paper. Figure 33 shows an unoverprinted 25c Juarez (Scott 127a) from this first 1879 printing. This copy has a special attraction for the collector — a hairline plate crack to the left, above the top of the design.

Between 1881 and 1883, new printings appeared on a much thinner wove paper. These printings included some color changes and new 12c and 24c denominations. Although listed separately, the Small Numeral stamps of 1882, Scott 146-149, belong to the foreign-mail issue too, and include two denominations not found in the Juarez series. These stamps have all the features of the earlier classic issues, including overprinted district names and consignment numbers. Again, the numerical overprints are a combination of an account number assigned to each of the various postal districts plus the last two digits of the year. The 2c and 3c values of the Small Numeral issue are shown in Figure 34.

Collecting the Juarez stamps presents the would-be specialist with a formidable challenge. Legitimately used copies are not rare, but are scarcer than one might suspect.

In those days there was not a great deal of foreign mail, and most of it emanated from the few Mexican port cities and towns of commercial importance. Low-denomination stamps from these places are not too difficult to find. Figure 35, for example, shows a 5c Juarez canceled with the datestamp of Veracruz. Although all of the smaller districts were issued Juarez stamps, use in many of these areas was extremely limited, and some are indeed extremely rare.

Higher denominations, particularly those above 25c, are also scarce to rare in used condition, even from the larger districts. Billings, who made a lifetime project of collecting these issues as well as the Hidalgo heads, noted that the busy seaport of Acapulco sold only 84 copies of the 100c stamp. Only one used copy has been recorded.

Covers bearing the Juarez stamps are highly prized by collectors and have become rather pricey. A spectacular array of them was seen at Ameripex 86, the international stamp show in Chicago, in Isaac Backal's Mexican maritime mail exhibit, which won a large gold award. The highlight of this group was a portion of a wrapper bearing 20 copies of the 24c Juarez, plus three stamps from other issues.

Unused Juarez stamps, both with and without overprints, are fairly abundant in certain denominations. At the expiration of the issue in 1883, relatively large stocks of unused remainders were returned to the main post office, and evidently most of these stamps eventually found their way into the stamp market. A few had been invalidated with pen cancellations. Unfortunately many of the clean stamps and those with overprints have since been used as raw material for favor cancellations or, in some instances, outright forgeries. Complicating the matter further is the fact that mute cancels were supposed to be used on the Juarez stamps. These are not too difficult to duplicate.

As the Scott catalog notes, the 1882 10c brown, 25c orange-brown and 85c red-violet on thin paper were never placed in use and will not be found with genuine overprints or cancellations.

Mexico's consignment overprint system provides some interesting varieties. For example, you occasionally will find a Juarez stamp with two consignment overprints, including one usually in red, and with perhaps two district names. This demonstrates an instance in which surplus stamps that were returned to the main post office were reassigned to another district.

Figure 36 shows one such stamp, referred to by collectors as a "habilitado" or revalidated stamp. This 1c thin-paper Juarez issue originally received the consignment overprint 3782 and

Figure 35. Although most Juarez stamps display mute cancels, this copy of the 5c has a Veracruz circular datestamp.

Figure 36. This revalidated or "habilitado" 1c Juarez stamp was first given the district name and consignment number for Guadalajara. It later was overprinted with a new number in red and the district name of Campeche.

Figure 37. A 24c Juarez shows a striking double transfer in its design, most notably in the top left corner of the stamp and in the left half of the value tablet.

Figure 38. A 1p Hidalgo Medallion of 1884, Scott 161.

Figure 39. Perf 11 Hidalgo Medallions, like this left-margin copy of the 10c stamp, are desirable.

"GUADALAJARA" district name. When it was returned to the post office, it was given a new 5083 overprint in red along with the "CAMPECHE" district marking for use there.

Many collectors are apt to be discouraged in their search for thin-paper Juarez stamps in good condition. This paper was very difficult to handle, so the majority of stamps were poorly perforated. Used copies generally suffered further deterioration when collectors soaked them off their covers.

The printing of the Juarez stamps, which was carried out in Mexico, was carefully done. The stamps represent examples of fine engraving and a high level of workmanship achieved at the government printing office. However, there are some fairly dramatic plate flaws to be found by the sharp-eyed collector, such as the plate crack on the 25c stamp in Figure 33 on page 24.

The 24c Juarez shown in Figure 37 displays another breathtaking variety, a remarkable double transfer at several points in the left of the design, most easily seen in the upper left corner of the stamp. Such flaws are worth looking for.

The philatelic literature on the Juarez issue is pretty skimpy. There are a few articles in the older issues of *Mexicana*. In 1937 Jose L. Cossio wrote and published a small monograph in Spanish on the Hidalgo and Juarez issues of 1874-83. I am unaware of any other such definitive works.

The Juarez issue, together with its contemporaries, the Hidalgo heads and Small Numeral stamps, marked the end of Mexico's era of district name and consignment number overprints. Although name overprints crop up on later stamps, Mexican postal regulations no longer required them.

These issues may not be to everyone's collecting taste, but I have found them to be interesting and not without great challenge and opportunity.

Hidalgo Medallion issues

If you love finely engraved postage stamps and are looking for a rather compact field in Mexican philately in which to specialize, you might want to consider the Hidalgo Medallion head stamps of 1884-85.

Except for denominations, the designs of all stamps in the series are identical. Each features a broad machine-engraved central oval containing the portrait of Father Miguel Hidalgo y Costilla facing left.

Figure 38 shows a 1p Hidalgo Medallion stamp. Within the machine work are the words "SERVICO POSTAL MEXICANO" (Mexican Postal Service) with the denomination spelled out. Numerals of value appear in boxes at all four corners of the stamp.

The stamps are somewhat larger than any previous Mexican issues, measuring about 25 millimeters by 31mm. A rather thin wove or laid paper was used to print them. While the paper accepted the printing impressions well, it proved very difficult to perforate with the equipment at hand.

The first series of Hidalgo Medallion stamps in 1884 had 15 denominations, ranging from 1c to 10p. The centavo stamps were printed in green and the peso denominations in blue.

In 1885 a second set of these stamps was issued in different colors, perhaps because 15 denominations in only two colors made it difficult to check for proper franking. These two issues mark Mexico's departure from the cumbersome system of district name and invoice number overprinting used on all previous issues. Still, a wayward district name may occasionally be found.

Although the Hidalgo Medallion issues were used for barely two years, there are enough varieties to provide considerable challenge in a specialized study. The vast majority of the stamps were perforated in gauge 12. However, most of the centavo stamps and the two low peso values also are encountered in perf 11. Figure 39 shows a left-margin copy of a 10c perf 11. These perf 11 stamps are much scarcer than the usual perf 12 and command a substantially higher price from a knowledgeable dealer. However, you can occasionally find one included among the cheaper stock.

There are also imperforate Hidalgo Medallion stamps, but heed the warning in the Scott catalog. These should be purchased in pairs or blocks since perforated singles with jumbo margins can be trimmed to make them appear imperforate.

Another variable that can be pursued by the specialist is color, especially among the green stamps of 1884. The late Abraham Odfjell, a famous Norwegian stamp collector who specialized in Mexico, found a correlation between color and time of issue. Early printings were generally bronze-green, the middle printings were green to dark blue-green, and the last stamps to be printed were sea green, the lightest shade of all. Odfjell noted that some shades were very scarce for certain denominations.

The perforating difficulties mentioned earlier mean that obtaining a well-centered, cleanly perforated example of any given denomination will require patience and a great deal of searching. Figure 40 shows a 12c stamp with typical perforations for these issues. Ragged edges and adhering blind perfs are the rule. This can be discouraging to the fastidious collector. But that's the way these stamps and many subsequent Mexican issues generally are found.

A glance at the Scott catalog listings will show that most of the centavo stamps and two of the peso stamps are valued from pennies to a few dollars. This makes it fairly easy to assemble a good showing of the Medallions without spending much money.

A more complete collection of the major varieties requires a considerable outlay. The two key items are the 5p and 10p stamps (Scott 230 and 231) issued later in 1892. They are printed on paper with the "CORREOS E.U.M." watermark. These two stamps are among a select group of true Mexican rarities seldom seen or offered for sale. The current combined Scott retail value for the pair in used condition approaches $4,000.

Other Hidalgos can be pricey, too. The 1c blue error of 1884 (Scott 150b) now lists at $275, but it hasn't risen as steeply in recent years as the 1892 blue-green rarities.

One anomaly of note is the apparent undervaluation of the 50c, 1p and 2p stamps of the first issue. The 50c value is shown in Figure 41. When issued, these three stamps would have been equivalent in face value to about 50¢, $1 and $2 U.S. But all of them are still cataloged at less than a dollar in unused condition or at $10 or under in used condition. I am not certain why this is so, but I suspect when the issue was superseded, there must have been thousands of remainders that were sold at deep discounts to dealers.

Figure 42 shows an 1896 flyer from a stamp dealer in Iowa offering perfect, unused copies of the 50c, 1p and 2p Medallion stamps for 20¢, 35¢ and 75¢, respectively.

The oval Hidalgo Medallion design also was used, without the rectangular frame and denominations, for Mexico's short-lived first Official stamps, Scott O1-9. This set was the only instance in which a

Figure 40. This 12c stamp displays the usual state of the perforations on these issues.

Figure 41. Higher-denomination 1884 stamps, such as this 50c (Scott 160), are believed to have come from large stocks that were remaindered when the stamps became invalid.

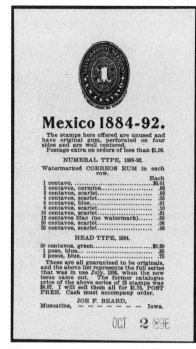

Figure 42. An 1896 price list suggests that large quantities of the 50c, 1p and 2p Medallions may have been sold to stamp dealers, explaining the stamps' relatively low catalog value today.

special Mexican stamp was produced for official correspondence. Subsequent Official issues consisted of regular postage stamps overprinted with the word "OFICIAL."

Contemporary Mexican postal cards and stamped envelopes also utilized the Hidalgo Medallion design. These are representative of the highest level of the engraver's art, and examples should be included in a specialized collection of the design.

There are many other interesting variations on these Medallion designs too, including printed private franks for Wells, Fargo & Co., Official envelopes, and wrappers for printed matter.

The most recent use of the Hidalgo Medallion occurred in 1968, when the design for the 1884 Official issue was used on two airmail stamps and an airmail souvenir sheet (Scott C333-34 and C345). These issues commemorated Efimex, the international stamp exhibition staged in Mexico City at the close of the 19th Olympic Games.

The Hidalgo Medallion head issues provide an opportunity for research and collecting in an area that, to my knowledge, has not received too much attention.

Large Numeral issues

Referring again to Figure 42, the advertisement was given to me by a friend as a philatelic souvenir. It is an envelope stuffer used by a 19th-century stamp dealer to call attention to then current Mexican stamp issues he had stocked for sale.

I never heard of Mr. Beard of Muscatine, Iowa, but the Large Numeral issue (Scott type A18) he was promoting offers some broad collecting opportunities. This is another series neglected by specialists. Literature on it definitely is lacking.

The Large Numeral definitives were used between 1886 and 1896. They were designed and produced at the government printing office using a machine-engraved oval frame with numeral centers designating the values.

Various colors, papers and perforations were employed, and this is the root of some of the problems collectors have had. There are many look-alike stamps with subtle, but important, differences. Even the listings in the Scott catalog are not altogether satisfactory, but they do form a basis for organization. In my view, the best system is to use paper characteristics as the primary means for grouping. E.W. Fager originally proposed this approach in an article he wrote in 1958.

Design dimensions, colors, and perforations are secondary characteristics in the organization. Here's how it goes:

For the first half of the period, from 1886 to about 1892, four different issues were produced on unwatermarked paper. The first stamps were printed on a hard, wove paper with clear designs about 28mm tall in the various colors listed from Scott 174 to 183. Dated cancellations show the greatest number were used in 1887.

Starting in 1887, stamps had blue lines on the face and/or the reverse. A paper shortage may have been behind this, as it appears surplus ledger sheets were used as printing stock. An example of a 10c stamp printed on this paper is shown in Figure 43.

This paper shows a clear wove pattern. Beware of the "blue-lined" stamps; fakes are many. Genuine lines are blue-green or dull green and, when viewed with transmitted light, appear quite bright, though sometimes almost invisible. Faked lines generally appear dark against transmitted light. Dated cancellations will favor 1888.

The next issue is found on a very soft paper with a faint, indistinct wove pattern. These are plentiful and relatively easy to identify with a little experience.

Many stamps of this issue have developed a yellowish cast, indicative of poor paper quality. On these, the oval is about 28.5mm high. Usage was between 1888 and 1891.

Still another coarse, soft paper can be distinguished for stamps of the same period. It is characterized by the presence of microscopic wood chips on the surface of the paper that are visible under strong magnification.

Dull colors are the rule with these stamps. The stamps are quite common but difficult to find in good condition. The paper stains easily and is so weak it tears readily. The oval design height is 28mm, which helps distinguish this type from other soft-paper stamps.

Between 1892 and 1896, there were at least two and possibly three distinct printings on watermarked paper. It is a hard-surfaced stock, with a clear wove pattern.

The stamps come in a variety of colors, much like the first series (with some exceptions). The Scott catalog lists them as 212-221.

The complete watermark pattern consists of 10 letters, CORREOSEUM, in 10 horizontal rows so that each stamp in the sheet usually shows all or part of one of the letters. Occasionally stamps belonging to these issues are found without the watermark. These come from the edge of the paper sheet, printed in a selvage area outside the watermark network.

Although listed by Scott in a separate grouping, the orange stamps are color varieties of this first batch. They were from early printings on watermarked paper and are found bearing postmarks dated 1892.

Another characteristic is the height of the oval, 28mm or slightly less, which differentiates this type from the final issue, which was printed on a thinner, hard, clear, wove paper. On these, the design oval is unmistakably taller, measuring 28.5mm or a fraction more.

A word about perforations: The normal perforation gauge for all stamps of this type was either 11 or 12. The existence of the 5½ and 5 and compound perf varieties is the result of difficulties with the perforating process. Examples of Numeral stamps with compound perforations are shown in Figure 44. Most experts now agree that the perforating machines consisted of comb-type devices with alternating long and short teeth. This was done to equalize the force needed to pierce the paper.

It is probable that several sheets were stacked for perforating at one time, and some of the sheets may not have been punched completely through.

Unfortunately, quite a few fabrications exist. I haven't yet men-

Figure 43. This 10c stamp was printed on ledger paper. It shows the faint blue-green lines on both the face and the back.

Figure 44. These stamps show the compound perforations frequently found on this issue. These are 5½ by 11 or 11 by 5½. Note the typical ragged edges from separation.

Figure 45. Mexico's Mulitas set gets its name from the design of the 4c and 12c stamps, which feature mules. Note the inscription at the foot of this 4c stamp. It refers to the government printing office.

Figure 46. Single letters from the watermark "CORREOSEUM" usually appear on copies of the Mulitas stamps if there is perfect alignment of paper during printing.

Figure 47. Due to misalignment, only parts of the "RM" watermark may appear on some Mulitas.

tioned the high-value 5p and 10p stamps issued on watermarked paper in 1892 (Scott 228 and 229). These are the keys to a complete collection and are very expensive, consistent with their scarcity. Even if your budget won't allow for these, you can still have fun hunting for the others and separating them into their proper categories.

It's a challenge to find nice copies of some of these stamps. Many have ragged perforations, poor centering and straight edges. The half-perf varieties are particularly difficult to locate in fine condition, since many were badly damaged when first separated from their sheets.

Mulitas issues of 1895-98

The 28th anniversary of General Porfirio Diaz' victory over French troops at Puebla in 1867 was April 2, 1895. Again, the Mexican post office chose this day to introduce a new series of stamps known as the Mail Transportation issue. It consisted of 13 denominations, from 1c to 10p, with five distinct motifs as the central designs.

Except for the 5c, these designs depicted various contemporary methods for the transport of mail. There is a foot postman with a knapsack, a mounted courier driving a pack mule, a stagecoach and a mail train. The oddball 5c pictures a statue of Cuauhtemoc, the last Aztec ruler of Mexico.

In the collector circles of Mexico, the stamps were affectionately known as the Mulitas. This is the Spanish word for small mules, which are in the vignette of the 4c and 12c stamps (shown in Figure 45). The designs were the result of a contest sponsored by the Ministry of Communications. Of several proposals, those submitted by an engraver named Gilbert Lomeli were selected as the most appropriate. His reward or prize is unrecorded.

In any event, the reaction to these stamps by the Mexican public was mixed. A contemporary journalist complained bitterly about the poor impressions, bad colors and tasteless designs. This, he said, was especially true of the 10c stamps. He lamented that the stamps were poor representatives of the people and government of Mexico to grace letters destined for foreign lands. He suggested a media crusade to have them withdrawn. We occasionally hear this same type of sentiment expressed in our own time.

For many years, the Mulitas were indeed considered a stepchild of philately by serious collectors. In the past few decades they have begun to receive considerably more attention. And well they should.

Casual inspection of the Scott or Minkus catalog listings confirms that they are an eminently collectible issue. The Mulitas have plenty of breadth and considerable challenge. Space here does not allow a lengthy discussion of the collecting possibilities, although one area that can be explored is watermark varieties. During the time the issue was current, papers with three different watermarks were used. When the stamps came out in 1895, they appeared on paper watermarked "CORREOSEUM." All or parts of the watermark characters are typically found on individual stamps, as shown in Figure 46. In 1896-97 the watermark was "RM" in interlaced script characters. A tracing of this watermark is shown in Figure 47. The stamps of late 1897 were printed on paper watermarked with an outline of the Mexican eagle with the letters "RM" beneath (Figure 48). Finally, the stamps of 1898 were printed on unwatermarked paper.

Further complications during production of these stamps led to even more collectible varieties in the form of mixed perforations. Normally the stamps were perforated 12, but combinations such as 12 by 6, 6 by 12 and even 6 by 6 are readily found. Most experts think these varieties resulted from defective perforating machines or improper operation of these machines. Both possibilities seem reasonable. Pairs imperforate between are not difficult to find.

Fortunately, there is now a great deal of specialized information available to anyone willing to tackle this issue. Numerous articles containing a wealth of information on the Mulitas have appeared over the past 20 years in *Mexicana*.

Many of the lower value stamps are not too expensive and generally can be found in retail stock books. Often one can purchase lots of unsorted stamps and enjoy looking for watermarks or elusive town cancellations. Sometimes older collections can be the source of misidentified varieties of a somewhat rare stamp, such as the 10c with sideways "CORREOSEUM" watermark.

Once a collector has worked his way through the Scott listings, he can begin looking for proofs and essays. Fortunately, a few of these items have survived in large, undivided pieces that are truly spectacular. *Mexicana* has illustrated these over the years. Sadly, most collectors will never be able to own these large proofs and essays, since they have become exceedingly expensive and change hands only among the wealthiest collectors.

One set that is near to the classification of proofs is definitely within reach of a serious collector. These stamps are known as the Black Mulitas. The set consists of a complete series printed in black ink (none of the Mulitas was normally printed in that color) on "CORREOSEUM" watermarked paper.

Most experts say the Black Mulitas were prepared as a presentation set for the Universal Postal Union but were also given to the diplomatic corps and notable Mexican politicians at the introduction ceremonies. The stamp shown in Figure 49 is from this set. It is identical in every respect to the issued stamps, except for the color.

Interestingly, the UPU did not accept these black stamps for its records, insisting instead that it be sent samples of the stamps in the colors of the normal issue. Whatever happened to the Black Mulitas originally sent to the UPU in Switzerland is not known.

However, in 1929 a surplus stock of these black stamps remaining at the post office was sold to dealers and collectors, and the stamps began appearing on the market. Probably not more than a few thousand sets of the Black Mulitas were printed. No one has yet discovered the records on these stamps. The Scott catalog does not list them, but the Minkus catalog does. In my view, they belong in a collection of this issue.

There are a few scarce stamps and one exceedingly rare stamp among the Mulitas. As one might expect, the peso denominations were mostly used for heavy or valuable parcels. Not many were printed or sold. From fragmentary postal records, it is estimated that about 50,000 1p stamps were sold and used. For the 5p and 10p values, the estimates drop to well below 5,000. These totals include all watermark types. It's anyone's guess what the survival rate was.

The rarest Mulitas stamp is the 1897 5p with eagle and "RM" watermark. It is doubtful that more than three or four sheets were printed. Fewer than a dozen have been confirmed genuine. An example is shown in Figure 50.

I vividly recall attending an international stamp show several years ago in which a large collection of Mexico was shown containing a splendid array of Mulitas. I was nearby when I overheard one of the judges ask to examine the 5p purported to be the eagle and "RM"

Figure 48. The Mexican eagle with the letters "RM" is the third type of watermark to be found on the Mulitas. It is often misaligned.

Figure 49. The Black Mulitas, such as this 10p specimen, were identical to the regular stamps, except that all denominations were printed in black. The mail train in this design is similar to those that carried mail between Veracruz and Mexico at the turn of the century.

Figure 50. The rarest Mulitas stamp, the 1897 5p with eagle and "RM" watermark.

watermark variety. The frame was dismounted and the stamp removed for inspection. Alas, it was not the rare variety, and I suspect the exhibit suffered severely from the attempted deception.

Definitive issue of 1899-1903

In 1991 two fortuitous finds piqued my interest in Mexico's definitive issue of 1899. Most collectors probably don't know that production of this final stamp issue of 19th-century Mexico (as well as that of the Independence issue that followed) was consigned to Bradbury, Wilkinson & Company, the well-known firm of engravers and printers in London, England. This is not mentioned in the Scott catalog; you must consult some of the foreign catalogs to determine this fact. The reason for farming out such an important government responsibility is not readily apparent. It could be that the regime of President Porfirio Diaz, which at that time was at the peak of its power, decided to curry favor with some of its British business friends who

Figure 51. Single colors were used to print the low values in Mexico's 1899-1903 definitive issue, including the 2c green (right) and 5c orange (far right) of 1903.

were investing heavily in Mexico.

It is also known, however, that the designs of the preceding 1895-98 Mulita definitives had not been popular in some quarters. This was explained in the Mulitas section. That issue had been the exclusive responsibility of the local government printing office.

The first seven stamps in the 1899 definitives, up through the 20c value, display the Mexican eagle coat of arms as the central design surrounded by different frames. Typical examples of these stamps are the monochrome 2c and 5c values shown in Figure 51. The four lowest values were printed in a single color, but the 10c, 15c and 20c were bicolored stamps. This meant that they were more expensive to produce, since two passes through the presses were required.

Figure 52 shows the design of the 20c rose and dark blue bicolor, Scott 300. It is fairly certain that a single master die was employed for the eagle in all the bicolored stamps, as this design feature is identical for all denominations below 50c.

The three top 50c, 1p and 5p values of the issue were large stamps of horizontal format portraying popular scenes in Mexico. The Salto de Juanacatlan, a waterfall near Guadalajara, is depicted on the 50c value. A view of Popocatepetl is the central design of the 1p stamp,

Figure 52. The 20c rose and dark blue bicolor, Scott 300.

and the National Cathedral is shown on the 5p high value. The 5p is illustrated in Figure 53.

In 1903 new printings of certain values were made, and a new denomination was added to the set. The colors of the 1c, 2c and 5c stamps were changed to conform to UPU requirements when Mexico modified its postal rates. The new denomination, a 4c stamp, was printed in red (or carmine, as Scott describes it), when such a value became necessary for certain domestic and foreign rates. The frame of the 10c stamp, a value mostly used to pay registration fees, was changed from violet to blue. There was also a subtle color change in the frame of the 50c stamp. The 1899 printings are a reddish lilac while the 1903 stamps are decidedly more red or carmine in color.

Genuine 50c stamps from the 1903 printing are definitely more elusive than their 1899 counterparts, a fact rightly reflected in their respective values.

Incidentally, both series are printed on a fairly hard, wove paper, diagonally watermarked in repeating parallel lines with the words "SERVICIO POSTAL DE LOS ESTADOS UNIDOS MEXICANOS." This watermark is usually visible by holding the stamps to a light or placing them face down on a dark background.

These stamps represent outstanding examples of the engraver's art and are a joy to examine under moderate magnification. The printing is first-rate, the perforations are clean and uniform, and the stamp impressions are usually very well-centered.

In themselves, the designs of the stamps are not remarkable. It appears that a single master die was made for the eagle holding a serpent in its beak, which serves as the central design for the seven smaller stamps, each of which has a different frame.

The subject matter of the three scenic views brings me to the fortuitous finds I mentioned earlier. Last spring I was browsing through a dealer's small stock of Mexican covers, when I came across a postcard mailed from Oaxaca, Mexico, to Belgium. It bore a transit marking, a strike of a Barr-Fyke "Recibida" machine cancel, which was used in Mexico City around the turn of the century. This caused me to take a second look. The cancellation ran over the edge of the card somewhat, but since I then did not own an example, the price was attractive enough that I bought it anyway.

Figure 53. This 5p high value of the series depicts the National Cathedral in Mexico City's main plaza.

Figure 54. This 50c stamp from Mexico's 1899 issue depicts a view of the Salto de Juanacatlan waterfall near Guadalajara as it is also shown on a turn-of-the-century picture postcard (left).

Only later did I examine the picture more carefully and realize that it was a photo of the famous waterfall near Guadalajara called Salto de Juanacatlan. The pictorial side of the postcard is shown in Figure 54. As I mentioned, the Juanacatlan waterfall was the subject of the 50c stamp in the 1899 issue, also shown in Figure 54.

A careful comparison of the stamp with the picture on the postcard convinced me that the photo from which the postcard was produced was probably used as the model for the engraved vignette of the postage stamp. Some of my collector friends argue there must have been hundreds of photos of this landmark. How could I be sure it was the one? Obviously, I cannot prove this to be the case. But I believe that the perspective, the breaks in the falling water and the plume of mist are too much the same to be mere coincidence. Unfortunately, the card lacks markings or inscriptions to identify who the publisher was.

A few months after I acquired the waterfall card I found another picture postcard, shown in Figure 55. This time the postcard scene is the one depicted on the 1p. There are three peasants and two burros in the right foreground of the postcard photo, and they have been faithfully engraved in exactly the same positions for the stamp design. There can be no doubt that the photo used for this card was the model for the stamp.

The Figure 55 card bears a number of inscriptions. On the face of the card is a description of the scene, "Mexico. El Popcatepetl." (one of the two dormant volcanoes overlooking Mexico City). Beneath that is the following: "111. Latapi y Bert. Apartado 922 Mexico."

It appears that this card is one of a series published by Latapi y Bert., a firm unknown to me. Printed in Spanish and French on the reverse is "Post Card" (at the top) and "Universal Postal Union" (one language along each side). There also is the admonishment that only the address may appear on that side.

Both postcards described here were used during the early years of the 1899 stamp issue. The waterfall card is dated November 1900, and the Popocatepetl card is postmarked November 1903. And, yes, both cards were franked with appropriate stamps from the 1899 Coat of Arms issue.

You can be sure I am searching for a contemporary postcard depicting the National Cathedral, the subject of the 5p stamp of this

Figure 55. The burros and peasants in the right foreground on this postcard showing an inactive volcano near Mexico City (right) establish the photograph as the design basis for Mexico's 1899 1p stamp.

Mexico.   El Popocatepetl.

111. Latapi y Bert. Apartado 922 Mexico

issue, to complete the set. The view of the cathedral on the stamp seems to be somewhat stylized, so perhaps I will not find a postcard with a perfect match. But I'll keep looking.

Serendipitous finds like these are perfect examples of why stamp collecting can be so much fun. I almost rejected the postcard with the Barr-Fyke cancel because the postmark was not complete. If I had, there could have been no story about the design model, or tracing the journey of the waterfall, which has given me as much satisfaction as acquiring an example of one of Mexico's earliest machine cancellations.

Curiously, this issue has not attracted the attention of many exhibitors, even though there are plenty of interesting avenues to pursue and there is a fair amount of rare material to search for.

Numerous proofs are available in both the colors of issue and many other shades. There are die proofs with the name of the printing firm inscribed beneath, and others with "SPECIMEN" perfins mounted on card stock. These items are so scarce that on those infrequent occasions when they appear at auction they attract spirited bidding. Some sell for hundreds of dollars.

The Scott catalog lists booklet panes for the 1903 1c, 2c and 5c printings. The catalog values for these items, shown in unused condition only, increased rather sharply about 10 years ago, but have since remained constant at $50 each. Prepared by hand from sheet stock, these booklet panes are actually much scarcer than the catalog would seem to indicate. A collector would be very fortunate indeed to obtain a pane at even two or three times today's catalog value.

About seven years ago, Bill Shelton, the noted San Antonio stamp dealer who specializes in Mexico, offered a previously unrecorded, unexploded booklet of stamps from the 1899 printing. It contained a pane of six 1c stamps and three panes of the 5c denomination, for a total face value of 96c. Shelton described the booklet as a major Mexican rarity and the only one known to him in his many years of selling Mexican stamps. I was told this booklet sold for $1,000 against an estimate of $1,250 to $1,500 — still a rather nice realization for a turn-of-the-century item from Mexico.

There are other rarities to be found as well. Dr. Karl Schimmer, a renowned specialist in Mexican philately, recently formed a nice exhibit of the 1899-1903 issues. He titled it "Mexico: Entering the 20th Century." In his search for unusual and scarce material, Schimmer found a wrapper fragment paying a 21c package rate to a foreign destination with a 20c stamp and a bisect of a 2c stamp. He is convinced that the bisect usage is legitimate. If so, this would certainly rate as an outstandingly rare usage in light of the fact that post offices nearly always had a large stock of 1c stamps on hand.

Around the turn of the century, various departments of the Mexican government used regular issues with "OFICIAL" overprints. It is interesting to note that Official stamps of the 1899-1903 issue appear with the "OFICIAL" overprint in two similar but slightly different type fonts. One consists of plain block letters of constant thickness, the other of letters that vary in thickness and have very small serifs. Both of these overprints are reproduced reasonably well in the Scott catalog's back-of-the-book listings of Mexico's Official stamps. Low-value stamps with the two overprint types are shown in Figure 56.

In all, 26 major varieties of Official stamps exist for the issue. They are cataloged as Scott O49-O74. For collectors who want a comprehensive collection, used Official stamps are somewhat elusive but relatively affordable, though a complete showing of all 26 in unused condition catalogs more than $1,500.

Figure 56. Subtle variations in the typeface used to supply the "OFICIAL" overprints mark these Official stamps as having been produced in 1900 (O49 top) and 1910 (O65 bottom).

But for those who would build a competitive exhibit of this issue, Official stamps must be well-represented on cover, too — a far more difficult proposition. Schimmer tells me that covers bearing these Official stamps are very difficult to find, and those with high values are next to impossible to locate. Generally, these would have been used on wrappers for packets or bundles of court documents, and such items are invariably discarded by the recipients.

All in all, the underappreciated Mexican definitives of 1899-1903 can provide the would-be specialist hours of enjoyment at a fairly reasonable cost, even though completeness may strain the pocketbook and require a lot of patience.

Chapter 3

Revolution and Civil Wars

The Torreon commemorative overprints

In the decade between 1910 and 1920, Mexico was racked with internal strife of a magnitude unmatched in this hemisphere since our own Civil War. Thousands of Mexicans lost their lives in this struggle, and the economic disruption was enormous. It was also a difficult time for the postal system. Provisional and local issues of stamps abounded, and the use of overprints and surcharges became the order of the day, depending on who was in power at any particular moment.

Casual inspection of the Scott catalog listings between numbers 321 and 607 reveals the extent of these civil war issues. And Scott lists only certain major varieties. This is another area of Mexican philately with plenty of room for specialization.

The first civil war overprint appeared in April 1914. To me it's one of the most interesting. It's called and is listed as the "Victoria de/ TORREON/ABRIL 2-1914" overprint used on the Transitory issue of 1914 (Scott 362-368). An example is shown in Figure 57.

The unusual aspect of this overprint is that its purpose was to call attention to a noteworthy military event. Most of the subsequent overprints had the function of validating or legitimatizing certain general issues for a particular region of the country under control of individual warring factions.

The Battle of Torreon, the subject of this issue, marked the emergence of guerilla fighter Pancho Villa as a bona fide military commander and a political figure to be reckoned with. The fascinating story of Villa's rise to power is too long and too complex to be summarized here. However, in the spring of 1914 he led a force of mostly peasant soldiers, known as the Division of the North, in an attack on the important railhead junction of Torreon. After a bitter fight, which lasted several days, he defeated a much better equipped Federal force and captured the town. It was an important victory for the Constitutionalist cause.

A holiday was declared in Ciudad Juarez, capital of the territory under Constitutionalist control. The postmaster, Ponciano Cota, was authorized to prepare the overprints to mark the event. The three-line overprint was applied by the Ellis Brothers print shop of El Paso, using a typeset form 10 subjects wide. The impression was repeated on each of the 10 horizontal rows comprising the sheet. The quality of workmanship was excellent. No errors are known, although an apostrophe-like speck appears after the "de" on the eighth stamp in each row.

Victoria de

TORREON

ABRIL 2-1914

Figure 57. The Torreon commemorative overprint. The measurements on genuine examples are: first line, 9.8mm by 1.5mm; second line, 8.5mm by 2mm; third line, 7.5mm by 1.5mm; separation between lines, 2mm.

Figure 58. These 5c and 10c Transitory stamps with the "Victoria de/TORREON/ABRIL 2-1914" commemorative overprint, used on piece, have the Ciudad Juarez circular datestamp cancellation. Virtually all legitimately used stamps bear this cancellation.

An example of the 5c and 10c overprinted stamps used on piece appears in Figure 58. The stamps are canceled with the Ciudad Juarez circular datestamp, which is typical of this issue.

The overprinted stamps were issued April 3 and sold only that day and the following day. The number issued was strictly limited, amounting only to a few sheets of the lower values in the series and a half sheet of the 20c and 50c values. According to the best information available (and this comes from contemporary stamp collectors), only three sheets (300 stamps) of the 1c, 2c, 4c and 10c denominations were prepared. Of the 5c denomination, some authorities say 10 sheets (1,000 stamps) were made. Others claim there must have been 15 sheets, citing the number of stamps actually seen.

As noted previously, only 50 copies of the 20c and 50c were overprinted, making these values the key stamps in the set. In any event, all of these stamps are scarce, but it's not too difficult to find examples of the 5c denomination.

An interesting variety of the 5c exists. The sheets of stamps used, which were rouletted for separation purposes, had a pair (positions 6 and 7) that were completely imperforate between. Stamps in positions 16 and 17 were rouletted only part way up from the bottom. So, depending on which number we accept, there can be only 10 or 15 such

Figure 59. A block of four of the 5c, imperforate between.

items. These can be considered rarities. A block of four with this variety is shown in Figure 59.

Some of the Torreon overprinted stamps were used on mail, both domestic and foreign. Nearly all legitimately used copies bear the circular datestamp cancellation of Ciudad Juarez, dated April 4. Complete covers are rare.

Unused stamps remaining unsold at the post office on April 4 were bought by an El Paso collector who, in turn, sold them to dealers and collectors for dispersal into the stamp market. Because of their scarcity, the overprints attracted the attention of counterfeiters, and forgeries do exist. Collectors should be wary of this when purchasing these stamps. Seek expert advice. If a set with the peso value is offered, be very suspicious. This denomination was not overprinted!

It is ironic that Pancho Villa, the man directly responsible for the battle victory that prompted this issue, was conspicuously absent from being honored on a Mexican stamp until 1978. Figure 60 shows the 1.60p Pancho Villa airmail stamp (Scott C568). Perhaps he was not honored because he was considered dangerous by the power brokers of his country. In the power struggle between 1917 and 1920, Villa's influence was neutralized. Finally, after some mischief in 1920, he was given a hacienda in Durango and went into self-imposed exile. Ultimately, he died as he had lived, in a hail of bullets from an ambush in the city of Parral as he rode through town in an open touring car with his bodyguards. The crime was never officially solved.

Figure 60. Although Pancho Villa played a dramatic role in the civil disturbances of 1913-20, he was not recognized on a Mexican stamp until 1978, when the airmail stamp shown here was issued commemorating the centennial of his birth.

Civil war-inspired overprints

The Torreon overprints marked the beginning of an era of overprints that, in some respects, rivals the complexity of overprinting seen on the early classic issues of Mexico. The overprinted, and later surcharged, stamps of the period 1914-18 are often referred to by Spanish-speaking collectors as "gomigrafos," which, roughly translated, means rubber-stamp overprints.

Many collectors are wary of embarking on a serious acquisition of these overprints because of the numerous manipulations that exist and the fact that many issues may have been created to meet philatelic demand. Still, for those with the patience and the motivation to do their homework, the stamps can become a fascinating study. A representative collection can be assembled without spending a lot of money. In fact, I have picked up several nice examples from dealers' shoebox offerings and remainder collections.

An increasing number of collectors have begun to specialize in these stamps recently. In 1983 MEPSI held its annual meeting in Hermosillo, Mexico, with an exhibition dedicated exclusively to the stamps of the revolutionary period. The good attendance and success of the exhibition indicated renewed interest in what once was an unpopular field. Mexico issued a special stamp (Scott 1311) to honor the event. It is shown in Figure 61. The stamp features a Sonora White Seal stamp (Scott 326).

The reason for so many different overprinted stamps can be understood readily when one reads the history of the Mexican Revolution. The movement began as a revolt against the government of Porfirio Diaz, which extended favors to the rich, but which exacerbated the plight of the peasants and working class. As the struggle wore on, various strongmen emerged, each in turn seizing control of the government. Internecine strife became the order of the day.

During this time, the postal system continued to operate (more or less), but the people in power saw to it that postage stamps bore the

Figure 61. Mexico issued this 6p stamp in 1983 to honor the Herfilex 83 stamp exhibition. It features a Sonora White Seal stamp.

Figure 62. These overprints were applied to Mexican stamps by various revolutionary factions.

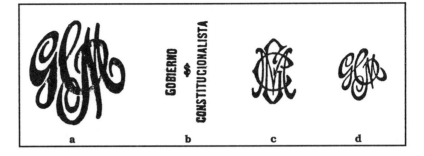

Figure 63. The government of Venustiano Carranza created these overprints.

Figure 64. Usually struck in violet or purple ink, large monograms were placed on 1910 stamps and a few of the 1899 issue. This type is referred to as the Hermosillo type.

40

mark of their party. As a result, numerous overprints were used to revalidate stocks of stamps left over from previous administrations.

The proliferation of overprints began in 1914, after the Torreon stamps. Most of these originated with the Constitutionalist movement in northern Mexico. The first was a large, rubber-stamped overprint with the interlaced letters GCM. An example is shown as "a" in Figure 62. Typically these overprints were struck in violet or purple on the then-current stamps of the 1910 issue. The GCM stood for Gobierno Constitucionalista Mexicano (Constitutional Mexican Government).

A variety of other overprints used in cities or areas under the control of revolutionary forces soon followed. Many of these never have been recognized by the Scott catalog but are listed in Minkus and other specialized Mexican catalogs.

The next Scott listings are for the so-called dollar-sign overprints (shown as "b" in Figure 62), where the words "Gobierno Constitucionalista" were typeset and applied to the 1910 series and to a few copies of the 1899 issue.

Two more common overprints were monograms. The overprint shown as "c" in Figure 62 is known as the Villa-type, ordered and applied at the end of 1914 during Pancho Villa's brief reign as supreme commander. The overprint "d" in Figure 62 is the Carranza type, used after Venustiano Carranza gained control of the government.

During Carranza's reign, there were additional overprints, as shown in Figure 63, often used in combination with the earlier ones. The overprint shown at the top of Figure 63 was a revaluation overprint. The "corbata" (necktie) type, shown at the bottom in Figure 63, designated still another form of government (which I believe stood for Provisional Government of Mexico).

Figures 64 through 67 show the various overprinted stamps. Figure 64 features a large monogram that was placed on 1910 stamps. Figure 65 features the dollar-sign overprint mentioned previously. Another example of an overprint of this period is shown in Figure 66. Figure 67 shows a combination of overprints used on one stamp. The 4c stamp shows the monogram overprint of the Carranza government and a "corbata" (necktie) overprint.

Some of these overprinted stamps are fairly common, but a few are scarce and have high catalog prices. Use caution when buying the scarce stamps. I've always thought these stamps should be collected used and on cover. Examples of such usages should be checked carefully to be sure the postmarks and the covers correspond to the correct usage period. In other words, they must be from towns and cities that were under control of the issuing entity.

The situation was so fluid in Mexico from 1910 to 1920 that control shifted rapidly from one faction to another. A good history book is essential to track these events.

Civil war local stamps

Another complication was that certain states and localities printed their own provisional stamps. Some of these are noted in the major catalogs; others are not. They too can be a lot of fun. Many types properly used range from scarce to very rare. For example, provisional stamps produced for Oaxaca, Sonora and Baja California were used on mail, but several of these stamps are difficult to locate. They fetch high prices when they appear at auction.

For example, the state of Sonora, where many of the civil uprisings began, issued several sets of local stamps. The first of these were the White and Green Seal issues, Scott 321-346. Examples are shown in Figures 68 and 69. These were followed by the Coach Seal issue, Scott 394-404, and the Anvil Seals, Scott 405-413.

There were further varieties, including a set overprinted for use in Baja California and another with the added word "Plata." The "Plata" overprint indicated that in an environment of monetary instability, the stamps were denominated in hard silver currency.

Far to the south, the revolutionary government of the State of Oaxaca issued local provisional stamps with a coat of arms. The catalog lists these as Scott 414-419.

With the exception of the scarce varieties of the early Sonora locals, it is not difficult to assemble a full complement of these stamps in unused condition. When they were no longer needed, unused stocks of these locals quickly found their way into the stamp market.

George Ward Linn, founder of *Linn's Stamp News*, is principally known for his philatelic news journalism, his stamp dealing and his life-long efforts to promote the hobby of stamp collecting. But Linn had a much more serious side in the true philatelic sense.

George Linn became infatuated with the Mexican War stamps, as he called them, and studied them seriously. The White and Green Seal stamps of Sonora (Scott 321-346) captured his attention. Linn, who is shown in Figure 70, formed an extensive collection of these stamps through connections he had in Mexico. No doubt there were commercial motives behind his acquisitions, as he later began specializing in the sale of Mexican civil war issues.

The result of his careful study was a book, *Mexico, The White and Green Seal Issues of Sonora*, which Linn wrote and published himself in 1916. It is still considered the definitive work on these stamps. Very little new or useful information has been added in intervening years.

Being a publisher himself, Linn was fascinated by the process used to print the Sonora stamps. A row of five typeset forms constituted the basic design and layout. This was imprinted twice on the paper, yielding a sheetlet of 10 stamps — five tete-beche pairs. (Tete-beche pairs are printed with one stamp inverted in relation to the other.) Subsequently, the sheets were sent through the press a second time to add, in red, the literal and numerical values plus the word "Correos."

Typographical mistakes and the use of different type fonts and styles created a host of varieties. At least two different kinds of watermarked paper were used.

To further complicate matters, after the printer delivered the stamps, the postal authorities decided some form of validation was necessary to guard against counterfeiting. This was accomplished by embossing the word "CONSTITUCIONAL" across the face of each stamp. These stamps are known as the White Seal stamps (shown in Figure 68).

Presumably because the embossing process consumed so much

Figure 65. This overprint type is nicknamed "dollar sign."

Figure 66. Another example of an overprint used during the civil war.

Figure 67. Combinations of overprints exist, such as this example overprinted with a monogram of the Carranza government and a "corbata" (necktie).

41

Figure 68. Invisible in this photo is the white embossing employed as a security measure on the Sonora provisionals.

Figure 69. The Green Seal issue.

Figure 70. A youthful looking George Linn.

time, postal authorities quickly adopted a different procedure for validation. A green facsimile of the seal of the State of Sonora was printed on each of the stamps. These stamps are the so-called Green Seal issue. An example is shown in Figure 69.

Because there were slight variations in each of the seal impressions, further varieties resulted. Linn studied and wrote about these different combinations.

The editors of the Scott catalog tried to list these stamps in a simple, condensed manner by assigning nine major varieties and eight subvarieties to the White Seal issue. Similarly, the Green Seals were assigned 11 major varieties and 12 subvarieties.

But as is often the case, these issues were not that simple. Despite the fact that Linn had brought attention to these issues very early in the game, the Scott catalog editors chose to ignore some of Linn's information. Mistakes in the Scott lists have remained unchanged for more than 70 years. The difference may not be too important to a general collector, but a specialist will certainly want correct information.

The details are in the Linn book. Linn lists the characteristics of the different printings, the typographical slips and the flaws in the seal overprints. Reproductions of all the sheets issued and the varieties on them are included in the back of the book.

Linn even outlined a detailed checklist of all the varieties known to him. This was a number in excess of 650. Many of these varieties are exceedingly rare, if they exist at all today.

For years, the Sonora stamps were not popular except among a handful of Mexican civil war buffs. However, catalog prices for the more elusive pieces have marched upward in recent years. The stamps seem to have become what Linn said they were more than 70 years ago — among the rarest stamps from Mexico.

I have no idea how many copies of the Linn book were originally printed. It is missing from the American Philatelic Research Library in State College. The book originally was printed on deckle edge rag paper, bound in an attractive paper cover. As can be seen in Figure 71, Linn had elegant cuts prepared for the chapter and page headings. Also note that he impishly autographed his photo (shown in Figure 70) "Sonoraly yours, George Ward Linn." He was about 32 years old when the book appeared, but he looks much younger in the portrait.

The book sold for $1 in 1917. MEPSI published a 24-page summary of the Linn book in 1971. It would be a matter of luck or diligent searching to find a copy of the original, but all the important information is contained in the MEPSI booklet.

Linn went on to engage in a rather brisk business involving the war stamps of Mexico. In 1917 he published another book describing many of the other wartime issues and giving collectors advice on how to collect them. Linn also was involved in a project to produce stamps for Mexico during the civil war era.

I like to collect used stamps — used, rather than merely canceled — and herein lies a problem. With an ample supple of cheap unused material available, how can one be sure that obliterated stamps actually performed the postal service for which they were intended? Many of these stamps did not, and the Scott catalog has recognized this fact with footnotes and italicized pricing. Favor or backdated cancellations are rather common for some of these issues, and one has to be careful to avoid them.

I look for stamps bearing enough of a cancellation so that location, date of mailing and cancellation type can be determined.

The White and Green Seal locals of Sonora were used extensively, and it isn't too difficult to find them with legitimate town or railway post office cancels. The examples in Figure 72 are readily seen to be correct usages with proper and largely complete circular datestamps.

The Coach Seal stamps also were widely used, but it is fairly obvious that the overfranked registered cover in Figure 73, which bears a complete set, was a philatelic creation even though it unquestionably passed through the mails. By contrast, the business letter in Figure 74 shows an example of a Coach Seal cover properly franked.

The Baja California set, Scott 401-404, is readily available in unused condition and is quite cheap. You will see purportedly used stamps from time to time, but the vast majority of these were made for the stamp trade and never did postal duty. The same is true for the Anvil Seals, Scott 405-409. The stamps with "PLATA" (silver) overprints were never officially put into use, but forged cancels abound. Unless you want to get deeply involved in the meticulous study of these issues, it might be safer to settle for unused copies of Scott 401-413.

The Oaxaca provisionals, Scott 414-419, have always intrigued me. As the catalog notes, these crude but quaint stamps were printed on backs of postal forms because of a shortage of paper. There is much more to the story of how these stamps came to be printed.

The Oaxaca locals bear the word "TRANSITORIO," which indi-

Figure 72. Postally used Sonora White Seal (far left) and Green Seal (left) issues created for use during Mexico's civil war.

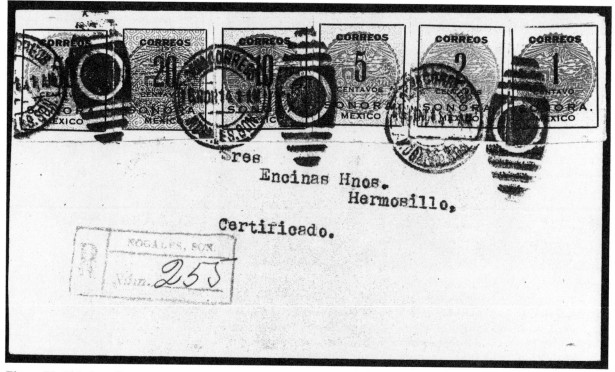

Figure 73. This heavily overfranked registered cover bears a complete set of Sonora Coach Seal stamps. It probably was prepared by H.C. Hopkins, an early student of Mexican philately who lived in Mexico during the civil uprisings.

cates they were meant to be a temporary expedient. However, records show they were valid for use from about June 1915 to June 1916.

It is apparent from reports of genuinely used copies that few of these stamps were in fact used to frank letters. Covers are very scarce, and many of the used stamps seen in the stamp market are believed to be canceled-to-order remainders. Here again, I look for stamps with enough of a cancellation to confirm the stamp's location and date of use, and even that may not be enough.

Figure 75 shows the two types of used 5c stamps from my collection. The type I with the thick "5" bears almost half of a railroad

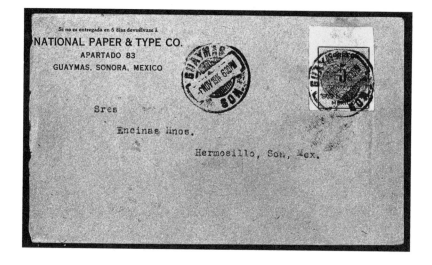

Figure 74. Also a Hopkins item, this single-franked commercial cover from Guaymas to Hermosillo with a 5c Coach Seal provisional went to the same addressee as the philatelic cover in Figure 73.

Figure 75. The thick "5" type I (far left) and thin "5" type II (left) 5c Oaxaca provisional stamps. The dated railroad agent's cancel on the stamp on the far left indicates that it was postally used, but too little of the date and design appear in the cancel on the left stamp to be certain. It is likely a canceled-to-order item.

agent's handstamp. It is dated within the authorized period of use, so I think it is probably an authentic cancellation. The other stamp bears part of a registry cancellation dated (19)16, but I can't be absolutely sure about it. I intend to keep looking until I find a copy with all or most of a properly dated town cancel.

You should be warned that the type I stamp with the thick "5" — the expensive variety — has been the object of a clever forgery. Copies of the common type II stamp have been altered by painting a thick figure directly over the thin figure "5" so that it appears to be a type I stamp. Usually, inspection under a strong glass will reveal such a deception. Also, remember that the type I stamp is somewhat darker in color, and that the eagle is more clearly defined than on the type II stamp. The majority of these counterfeits are the work of Raoul de Thuin, a prolific forger who moved to Merida on Mexico's Yucatan Peninsula in 1931. De Thuin specialized in forgeries of Latin America in general and Mexico in particular.

Figure 76 shows the only Oaxaca provisional cover in my collection. It took me a long time to find one.

Figure 76. An Oaxaca provisional stamp on cover. The 1c rate is for a local drop letter (Ciudad=City). Because of its small size (104mm by 66mm), this probably carried a lady's note or party invitation.

If you want a challenge in Mexican stamps, the civil war locals will provide you with one. Try to find as many legitimately used civil war locals as you can.

Civil war-era mixed frankings

From time to time, I encounter covers from the Mexican civil war era that bear stamps of two different issues, and even covers addressed to the United States with U.S. stamps in addition to those of Mexico. These certainly can be interesting additions to one's collection. But sometimes the explanation of why these mixed frankings came into being is elusive.

The cover shown in Figure 77 is a case in point. It is a mourning letter from Magdalena, in Sonora state, to Los Angeles, franked with a 5c Transitorio stamp (Scott 369). These stamps came from a shipment of samples that a youthful George Linn sent to the rebel Constitutionalist government in his quest for a printing contract to produce their postage stamps.

The explanation of why the cover in Figure 77 also bears a 2¢ U.S. postage due stamp is fairly simple and straightforward. When the letter crossed the border into the U.S. mail system, the Transitorio stamp was judged not to be valid for international mail, so the item it franked was treated as an unpaid letter.

This handling is typical for many of the so-called local issues, particularly those of northwestern Mexico. These locals were produced by various factions seeking to unseat the Federal group then in control of the government and in response to stamp shortages that developed when regular stamps could not be obtained from Mexico City.

Mexican locals, such as Sonora's White Seals and Green Seals (321-346), the Transitorios (354-361), the Denver Eagles (386-393) and many of the later civil war overprints, had not gone through the validation procedures prescribed by the Universal Postal Union.

There were no specific directives from the U.S. Post Office Department in Washington, D.C., regarding these issues, so U.S. postmasters along the border were more or less on their own in deciding whether to accept or reject such franking. Many opted for the latter. There was, of course, no problem if letters bore stamps of

Figure 77. Because the 5c Transitorio was a local issue produced for Mexican rebels, it was not recognized as legitimate franking on this 1914 mourning cover to Los Angeles. The addressee was assessed 2¢ postage.

Mexico's 1899, 1903 or 1910 issues. These were still valid for postage — if anyone had a supply of them.

Naturally, there were exceptions to this practice of non-recognition. Occasionally, letters franked only with Mexican local issues went through the international mails unhindered. Figure 78 shows an example of this in the form of a 1914 registered letter to Germany with a 20c Transitorio paying 10c for the foreign rate and the 10c registry fee. A backstamp, also shown in Figure 78, attests to the fact that this letter crossed into the United States at Nogales, Arizona, and cleared the New York foreign-mail office on its way abroad. But I have seen many similar letters where the Transitorio stamps were not recognized.

Mexican mailers of that period tried to cope with these problems in several different ways. Some reverted to a method of forwarding, sending their U.S.-bound letters to friends or agents living on the border who would carry them to a U.S. post office, affix U.S. stamps and send them on their way. Others were able to secure a small supply of U.S. postage stamps to use in combination with their local stamps, relying on the locals to get their letters to the border and the U.S. stamp to carry them beyond. This practice produced mixed frankings, even if one of the stamps could be said to have had limited postal validity.

The cover illustrated in Figure 79 demonstrates this method. I believe it is safe to assume that the sender of this cover had 2¢ U.S. stamps, which were used in combination with the Sonora locals, in this

Figure 78. Though many such usages were assessed postage due, this 20c Transitorio cover was accepted and passed serenely through the U.S. mails on its trip to Karlsruhe, Germany. The sender, A.O. Tittman, was another noted collector who lived in Mexico at the time.

47

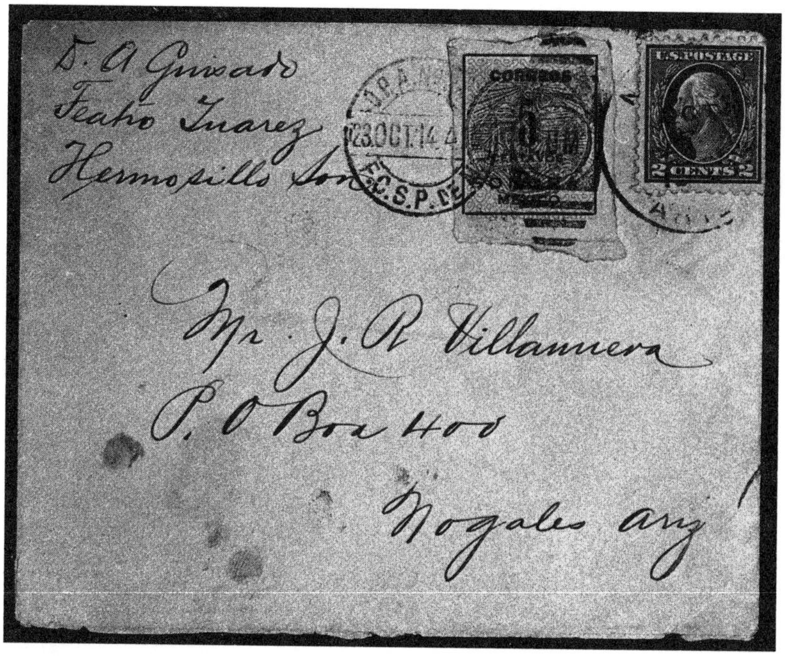

Figure 79. This cover demonstrates the mixed-franking practice. The sender of this cover used a 2¢ U.S. stamp in combination with the 5c Sonora local stamp to assure undelayed delivery to the addressee in Nogales, Arizona.

case the 5c Coach Seal, to assure undelayed delivery to the addressee in Nogales, Arizona.

Figure 80 shows a cover that displays yet another way to solve the problem. This letter from Chihuahua to the British ambassador in Washington bears two 5c stamps: one of Mexico's 1910 Independence issues (Scott 314) and a 1914 5c Denver Eagle (Scott 389). There is a temptation to say that this cover represents a double-letter rate, requiring 10c postage. But I am convinced that the writer was simply covering all the bases, ensuring that a letter of some importance to him would reach its destination.

Since the Constitutionalists were in control of the state of

Figure 80. The combination of a 1910 Federal stamp (Scott 314) and a Denver Eagle local used by rebels in Chihuahua (Scott 389) assured normal handling of this 1914 letter sent to the British embassy in Washington, D.C.

Chihuahua, they were certain to recognize their own stamp (the Denver Eagle) as valid for domestic carriage as far as the U.S. border, even if they didn't like the Federal stamp. At the border, U.S. postal officials would honor the 1910 5c stamp, which had been recognized by the UPU.

There are many combinations of the usages described here to be found, which should make the search most interesting. Better still, such items are not so scarce that they are beyond the reach of a collector of modest means.

This situation with Mexico's locals probably spanned a period of about three years, from 1913 to 1916, so there should be plenty of material floating around for the informed and persistent buyer.

Regular issues of 1916-20

One of the 20th-century issues of Mexico I have felt would be fun to study in-depth is the regular issue of 1916-20 (Scott 608-628). The lower denomination stamps have the theme of famous men, mostly heroes of the revolution. The three top denominations, 40c, 1p and 5p, are in a larger horizontal format and show a map of Mexico, the lighthouse at Veracruz and the main post office in Mexico City.

The stamps remained in use for about seven years in the post-revolutionary era. The earliest printings, except for the 40c, 1p and 5p, were sold in rouletted form and were printed on a soft, thick unwatermarked paper.

I have never discovered exactly when this series was made available for public sale. Most catalogs show the date 1916, but stamps and covers with 1916 postmarks are difficult to find. There was severe inflation in Mexico during the latter half of 1916. Postal rates were raised several times, and there was widespread use of surcharges on earlier stamp issues. This may partially account for the scarcity of this issue used during its first year.

In any event, most of the rouletted stamps are plentiful and quite inexpensive in used condition. Only the imperf-between pair of the 5c and the unused 20c and 30c stamps will take a significant nip at your pocketbook.

I have found numerous shades for many stamps in the series, so this would be a good area to explore. The perforated stamps (Scott 618-625) represent a greater challenge.

It is reported that there was a small early printing on thin paper. This thin paper presented some handling difficulties for the post office, so a switch was made to medium-to-thick paper. The stamps printed on thin paper, at least the 1c to 10c denominations, were turned over to the philatelic office for sale to collectors. As a result, used copies of these stamps are considered to bear mostly favor-cancellations.

The high-value stamps are readily found on thin paper. Since fewer of these were required in the normal shipments, they did not present the handling problems the low denominations did.

A key stamp in the perforated series is the 3c brown, showing a portrait of Jose Maria Pino Suarez, a martyr of the revolution. A copy of the stamp is shown in Figure 81. This has always been a difficult stamp, in stark contrast to the rouletted 3c, which is one of the most common stamps of that series. I do not have a good explanation for this.

In 1917, when the 3c was issued, postal rates had been restored to more normal levels after a year of inflation. But rates were such that there really wasn't any great need for a 3c stamp. There may have been ample inventories of the 3c rouletted stamp on hand.

Collectors should exercise caution when purchasing a 3c perfo-

Figure 81. The perforated 3c value is one of the key stamps in the 1916-20 definitive series.

Figure 82. This 1p features the central post office, the vignette that normally appears on the 5p. The 5p shows the Veracruz lighthouse, the vignette that should appear on the 1p.

rated stamp. There have been instances where large-margin copies of the rouletted stamp have been perforated to resemble the scarce ones. Obtain a reliable certificate or examine the stamp carefully under high magnification to make sure there are no traces of roulette marks on the perforation tips.

The perforated 20c and 30c stamps in unused condition are difficult to come by, too, and should be acquired with care.

The 1p and 5p stamps provide some remarkable varieties. Both stamps were designed to be bicolor, requiring two separate printing operations. An error occurred during the printing. As a result, the 1p is known with the vignette of the 5p, the central post office. The 5p is known with the Veracruz lighthouse as its center. Examples are shown in Figure 82. There has always been some suspicion that these were more than just pure accidents.

The other variety the Scott catalog lists for the 1p is one of my favorites, the blue frame with a somewhat darker blue vignette. Scott formerly cataloged this stamp as number 627, a major variety. They have since renumbered the series between the 4c and 5p so that the blue-on-blue variety is now listed, and correctly, I believe, as 627b. The stamp is an error. Examples of the blue-black stamp and blue-on-blue variety are shown in Figure 83.

The blue-on-blue variety is not difficult to find in used condition, and well-centered copies are easily within reach of most of us. But a genuine unused blue-on-blue is quite another matter. When I was searching for one many years ago, several times I was presented with examples of the normal stamp, blue frame, black center. Usually the vignette was weak or somewhat underinked so that it appeared to take on some of the bluish color of the surrounding frame. But inspection under a strong glass always resolved this false perception.

Eventually a good one was found, but it required a bid very near full catalog. I have always considered this to be one of the dozen or so really difficult 20th-century Mexican stamps. Its catalog value has risen six-fold in the past 20 years, and that pretty much tells the story.

Figure 83. The normal blue-black 1p stamp is shown at right. An example of the blue-on-blue variety is shown at far right.

50

Besides the color shades mentioned earlier, there are numerous other collectible varieties. As noted in the Scott catalog, the 10c stamp comes with and without imprint at the base of the design. The 40c stamp has been reported without imprint, but I have never seen one. The 5p stamps were sometimes overprinted with control numbers, usually in red or violet. An example is shown in Figure 84.

The rouletted series is available imperforate, but a collector should purchase only pairs and examine the space between the impressions very carefully. If traces of roulette indentations are found, it is not imperforate.

Double entries and other engraving mistakes are reported for the 1c and 2c denominations. I suspect there may be other minor plate flaws for those who enjoy looking for them. Devotees of postal history could certainly have some fun looking for early usage and unusual rates for this issue. I have only a couple of stamps that, from cancellations, I can positively ascribe to 1916.

Figure 84. A poorly perforated example of the 5p 1917-20 printing with control number overprint (Scott 628a).

Chapter 4

Modern-era Stamps

Pro-Universidad stamps of 1934

The modern Pro-Universidad issue has always been a 20th-century favorite of mine from the standpoint of beauty and workmanship. The Pro-Universidad issue consists of a 10-value set for regular surface mail and eight airmail stamps. The stamps were issued to raise money for the University of Mexico. The principle behind these stamps was not too different from that of the semipostal stamps European countries were issuing to support worthy causes.

The world was in an economic depression, tax revenues were suffering and a stiff deficit had been forecast for the school. But despite hard times, stamp collecting remained an extremely popular pastime. Affluent collectors seemed ready to buy almost any attractive and well-executed stamp set that came on the market.

The subjects of the 10 stamps in the regular-mail set are indigenous Mexican crafts and ceremonial poses. Many collectors do not realize that these motifs are not original with this issue. They were copied from contemporary Mexican revenue stamps, often with only minor changes. The 40c and 50c stamps in Figure 85 were clearly derived from the corresponding revenue issues shown alongside them. Adapting their designs from revenues unquestionably reduced the time and cost of producing these stamps.

The designs for the Pro-Universidad airmails feature popular Mexican scenery, such as mountains. An airplane was worked into each design, though often in an awkward flight position.

It is worth noting that the three peso-denominated issues of the regular-mail set and all but one of the airmail stamps are bicolor. The printing registration for the frames and vignettes is almost perfect in all copies I have seen.

Both sets were a strictly limited edition. Except for the 1c, 5c and 10c surface-mail stamps, printing quantities of the rest of the denominations were 50,000 or less. A complete rundown of the numbers issued appears in the chart in Figure 86. The rationale for these low quantities was that collectors and dealers would snap them up in hopes of quick appreciation in value and perhaps a fast profit. Only 1,000 copies of the 10p surface-mail stamp were issued, and but 1,500 of the 20p airmail stamp. Both high values sold out almost immediately. It was reported that the 10p surface-mail stamp was sold out at 10 a.m. on the first day of sale.

At that time, the Mexican peso was worth hundreds of times more than it is today, so the 1934 cost at the post office for the two top values

Figure 85. The designs of Mexico's 40c and 50c Pro-Universidad stamps (far left) were adapted from those of two Mexican internal revenue issues of 1930 (left).

came to sightly more than $8.50 U.S. — quite a bit of money for the Depression era.

But Mexican authorities had already taken a step that guaranteed at least partial success to the venture. It had been decreed that between September 1, the day the stamps were released, and Decem-

1934 Pro-Universidad — Number of stamps issued			
Surface mail		**Airmail**	
Scott number (value)	**Quantity issued**	**Scott number (value)**	**Quantity issued**
697 (1 centavo)	20,000,000	C54 (20c)	50,000
698 (5c)	1,000,000	C55 (30c)	20,000
699 (10c)	2,000,000	C56 (50c)	10,000
700 (20c)	50,000	C57 (75c)	10,000
701 (30c)	30,000	C58 (1p)	10,000
702 (40c)	20,000	C59 (5p)	3,000
703 (50c)	10,000	C60 (10p)	2,500
704 (1 peso)	10,000	C61 (20p)	1,500
705 (5p)	2,000		
706 (10p)	1,000		

Figure 86. Except for the lowest three values of the surface-mail stamps, the printing quantities of Mexico's 1934 Pro-Universidad issue were extremely limited, as the table indicates.

Figure 87. Mexico's 1934 Pro-Universidad 1c stamp was part of a set issued to raise funds for the University of Mexico. Success of the issue was aided by a ruling that the 1c stamp in the series would be required on all letters sent between September and December 1934.

ber 31, 1934, all domestic letters were to bear a 1c Pro-Universidad stamp in addition to the regular franking. A copy of the 1c is shown in Figure 87. I am reasonably confident this rule wasn't rigorously enforced, but collectors frequently find covers from this period with the extra stamp. Figure 88 shows a slightly unusual usage of the 1c, added not to a domestic letter but to a commercial airmail cover from Michoacan to Chicago.

The printing of the 1c stamp was so large that it is almost always present in a general Mexican collection, sometimes accompanied by the 5c and 10c stamps as well. By contrast, there is a subvariety of the 10p regular issue that is printed on unwatermarked paper. It is easily the scarcest of the Pro-Universidad issues, since it is believed that only one sheet of 100 originally existed. An example of this rarity is shown in Figure 89.

As one would expect with any set of stamps available in such limited quantities, catalog prices can be volatile. From the early 1960s, when I began specializing in Mexico, to the early 1980s, the catalog value of these stamps rose tremendously. The two high values increased by factors of six times and 20 times, respectively. Since then, prices have slipped, reflecting the general slump in the stamp market. For example, the 20p airmail stamp, which peaked at $2,000 unused in 1982, fell to $1,100 in the 1990 Scott catalog listing, when prices were adjusted to reflect the prevailing market values. The 10p surface-mail stamp reached its zenith of $1,400 a little later, but settled back to $1,000 in 1990. But that rare, unwatermarked subvariety, Scott 706a, just keeps climbing. It now lists for $3,250. There has been no movement in these listings for the past few years.

It has been my experience that Pro-Universidad sets may sell at auction for some discount below the catalog value. But fresh, well-centered mint or very lightly hinged copies often command a respectable 80 to 100 percent of their catalog values.

If you do not yet own these sets and are keen on having them, it is wise to be patient and search for the best quality you can find. Centering is often a problem, especially with the 1p surface-mail stamp, the design for which is about 1mm wider than all the other stamps in the set. It is difficult to find copies where the perforations do not cut the frameline on one side or the other.

Beware also of multiple hinging. Many Pro-Universidad sets moved between albums several times before the era of hingeless

Figure 88. This 1934 cover from Michoacan to Chicago bears a 1c Pro-Universidad stamp to comply with a postal decree.

54

mounts, with each new owner applying a fresh hinge. Regumming does not yet seem to be a big problem with this issue, although it can occur.

Collectors of used stamps will find it extremely difficult to complete sets in that condition. Most were collected unused. Of the surface-mail stamps, only the 10p value catalogs more used than mint. The reverse is true for all but one of the airmail stamps. Check closely to make sure that cancellations are contemporary with the period of issue. Stamps with heavy hinging or spoiled gum are raw material for fakers tempted to add modern cancels.

It is doubtful that the top denominations of either set were ever used on anything other than philatelically contrived covers. They represented too much postage for normal, everyday mail rates.

I like the Pro-Universidad stamps. They represent some of the best designs and engraving work to come out of Mexico during the 1930s. They may seem a bit expensive for the average collector, but there is little doubt that the Pro-Universidad stamps are one of the most popular Mexican issues with serious collectors around the world.

I believe these stamps represent a sound philatelic property.

Architecture and Archaeology series — surface-mail stamps

The group of stamps used by Mexico between 1950 and 1975 is usually referred to as the Architecture and Archaeology series. While this description pretty well covers the range of subjects chosen for the stamp designs, there were exceptions, especially for some of the surface-mail stamps.

As shown in Figure 90, two Mexican patriot leaders, Benito Juarez and Francisco Madero, were portrayed on the 15c and 10p stamps of the issue. Juarez is also seen on a 50p stamp issued late in the period.

As in the current Exporta series, many of the designs of early Architecture and Archaeology issues remained in use virtually throughout the life of the series. Figure 91 shows a good example: two stamps depicting La Purisima, a modernistic church in Monterrey. The 3c stamp on the top was introduced in 1951. Its 3p counterpart on the bottom was released in 1975.

It also must be noted that a short set of stamps (Scott 897A-900) issued in 1956 to honor the centennial of the Mexican constitution is customarily included in collections of this issue. Figure 92 shows the

Figure 89. The rarest stamp in the Pro-Universidad regular-issue set is the unwatermarked variety of the 10p. Only one sheet of 100 is believed to have been printed.

Figure 90. The Architecture and Archaeology series also includes stamps depicting Mexican patriots, such as Benito Juarez and Francisco I. Madero.

Figure 91. The 1951 3c stamp on the top and the 1975 3p stamp on the bottom feature the same design depicting a church.

three designs used. These stamps were issued in denominations needed to meet specific new rates. In addition, there was no presidential decree limiting the quantities of these stamps to be printed, as is customary with Mexico's commemoratives. Further, new denominations of these Constitution designs were issued at later dates.

All of these surface-mail stamps were printed in a small format, with the designs measuring roughly 17mm by 20mm and overall stamp dimensions of 20mm by 24mm. Two printing processes were employed. In the early printings, the photogravure process was used for denominations up to 50c. Engraved plates were produced for the peso values. By the end of the 25-year time span during which these stamps remained in service, all values were being printed by photogravure.

As expected, the numerous printings give rise to a rich range of colors and shades, and there are plenty of minor plate and printing varieties to add excitement to the hunt.

With very few exceptions, the surface-mail stamps were perforated in gauge 14. The three that were not are perf 11: a 1p stamp produced in 1958 (Scott 822b) and two 1969 coil stamps that are perf 11 vertically (Scott 1003-04). Examples are illustrated in Figure 93.

A number of different papers figured in the production of these stamps, and this has been the basis by which many catalogers and collectors categorize stamps of the series. These characteristics will be discussed in detail in the following sections.

In about 1966, light-active components were incorporated into the manufacture of Mexican security paper in the form of optical brighteners and phosphorescent coatings. These characteristics can help one sort out the later printings. Finally, in the printings of 1975 — the last hurrah for the series — watermarked paper was abandoned.

The greatest challenge facing a collector who aspires to form a collection of this definitive issue is how to best organize it. The Scott catalog listings are somewhat confusing since the chronology of the series gets mixed up and the differences in light-active properties of the late printings are completely disregarded. British and European catalogers and album makers are better in this regard.

Lighthouse is my personal choice for a preprinted album. The Lighthouse publisher has sorted out all the nuances in papers, gums and light-active aspects of the Architecture and Archaeology stamps.

Figure 92. Though they were issued in 1957 to mark the centennial of the Mexican Constitution, these similar designs were used for almost two decades thereafter.

56

Figure 93. The only Architecture and Archaeology regular stamps not perf 14 are the 1958 1p stamp at left and two 1969 coils, including the 40c pair at right.

Another advantage to Lighthouse is that the regular, airmail, special delivery, postal insurance and parcel post stamps are all grouped together in the chronological album sequence.

In 1984 there appeared a special supplement to the journal of the Asociacion Mexicana de Filatelia, A.C. (AMEXPHIL), which deals with the Architecture and Archaeology series in meticulous detail. This study, written by Ignacio A. Esteva M., divides the total series into 11 distinct issues plus the Constitution stamps. With full-color illustrations, Esteva notes the key characteristics of the stamps in each issue. If you can read Spanish, this study is a good resource, especially if you plan to mount your stamps on blank album pages. There are no prices given, but the scarce and rare varieties are noted.

Even though the Scott listings are deficient in defining all the varieties that would attract the attention of a specialist, they do give some idea of the collecting possibilities.

Regardless of how one organizes his collection, there is much to look for. Colors and shades and printing and paper varieties combine to make for an exciting search.

Certain denominations of the early printings are becoming difficult to find. For example, the 20c Puebla Cathedral stamp of the first printing, which paid a common domestic rate, is quite cheap as a used stamp but rather expensive in unused condition. Most of the high values of all printings have exhibited firm pricing in dealers' stock books from the beginning. While it is a temptation to defer their purchase in favor of the more abundant cheaper varieties, these high values are the stamps that climb even higher in catalog value and retail price year by year.

Architecture and Archaeology airmail series of 1950-76

Another modern Mexican issue that lends itself to philatelic studies in the traditional sense is the definitive airmail series of 1950-76. It is made to order for a modern specialist, with collecting challenge comparable to a 19th-century classic issue.

Again, the main reason for the broad collecting potential is the long time span in which these stamps saw service and the numerous changes in the production schemes and postal rates in the period.

Figure 94. An example of the complexities of the long Architecture and Archaeology series can be seen in the 35c denomination of the first issue of 1950. At right is the original 35c stamp. At far right is the later version of the stamp printed from a retouched die.

Figure 95. This 1971 2p stamp features the same view of Taxco, state of Guerrero, that appeared on the 35c stamp of 1963.

Figure 96. This watermark was used for the earliest stamps of the Architecture and Archaeology definitive stamp series.

There is a more or less uniform design to the airmails. They all have a horizontal format (about 40mm by 24mm) with the value tablet occupying the left two-fifths of the stamp and a selection of historical, architectural or cultural subjects filling up the balance of the stamp. Even the ever-present Miguel Hidalgo, leader of Mexico's independence struggle, was chosen as the subject of the 10p stamp.

There were 13 denominations in the first series, starting with 5c and running all the way to 20p. This, combined with different papers, watermarks, retouches to printing dies, color shades, a variety of perforations, and the later addition of new denominations to old designs, makes the search for completeness quite exciting. Figure 94 shows a 35c stamp from this series. Shown on the left is the original version of the stamp; on the right is the retouched-die version.

Figure 95 shows a 2p stamp issued in 1971. It features the same design, a view of Taxco, that appeared on a 35c stamp issued in 1963. This is an example of how designs were reused, adding to the confusion of this issue.

Often bewildered by the apparent disorder in the Scott catalog listings of these stamps, collectors wonder how best to organize their collections. Perhaps the following notes will help. They are mostly a matter of chronology and the evolution of printing methods to meet the need for stamps.

The earliest emissions in 1950-52 all came from engraved plates printed in sheets of 30 on flatbed presses (Waite design) on pregummed paper of Mexican manufacture and watermarked "GOBIERNO MEXICANA" with the Mexican coat-of-arms eagle in a circle. (A tracing of this watermark is shown in Figure 96.) A sheet perforator of 10½ by 10 was used for the output from this press, and Arabic gum was used as the adhesive. The gum has a varying yellowish cast to it. In fact, this characteristic makes it easy for one with a practiced eye to distinguish these stamps from other, similar ones. The Scott catalog lists the 1950-52 stamps as C186-C198 with varieties.

In 1953 the Mexican bureau of printing began using a new supply of paper of British manufacture. This paper had a different watermark, "MEX-MEX" and the national emblem. A tracing appears in Figure 97. The circles around the eagle outline were incomplete and were intersected by the first and last letters of "MEX-MEX."

This paper came in various thicknesses, and sometimes the watermark is hard to discern. This paper also was used in the flatbed (Waite) presses and produced the stamps listed as Scott C208-C217. The watermark is horizontal, and the stamps are perforated 10½ by 10. Figure 98 features one of the key stamps in the series, the 50c printed on "MEX-MEX" watermarked paper.

In about 1955, another type of press, a rollfed Wifag rotary, came into service to print the airmail stamps. It could accommodate either recess-engraved or photoengraved plates. It had an 11 by 11 and an

11½ by 11 perforator associated with it and so contributed to the many varieties in the Scott listings between C218 and C221. Plate size was 50 subjects, and the press cylinder held three plates.

At this point in the chronological sequence, we must introduce another issue that belongs in the series, even though many stamp collectors refer to the stamps as a commemorative issue.

These stamps portray men involved in the drafting and passage of the constitution of 1857. The stamps are listed in the Scott catalog as C236-C237A. No presidential decree ever gave the stamps commemorative status, and they were reprinted numerous times and even underwent denomination changes when postal rates were modified. Figure 99 shows two of these stamps.

In the early 1960s, still another printing press (a Goebel) saw action printing airmail stamps. This coincided with a new supply of paper of American manufacture. The paper was thick, bore a tropic-resistant PVA (polyvinyl alcohol) gum and came with a new watermark design, an interlocking pattern of "MEX" and eagle in circles of larger diameter than the two previously mentioned. A tracing of this watermark is shown in Figure 100.

The Goebel press handled only photogravure plates and had a perforation of gauge 14 associated with it. The press made numerous high-speed printings as demand for certain denominations increased.

Scott listings of C265-C268 and C285-C298 show a mixture of engraved and photoengraved stamps, the photoengraved stamps being on the U.S.-made paper.

By the mid-1970s, with inflation rampant in Mexico, postal rates rose rapidly, necessitating stamps with odd denominations. The issue of 1975, Scott C444-C451, provided for these rates, including a 50p airmail, the highest airmail value issued up to that time.

The last stamps of the 1950 designs came out in 1975-76, when eight denominations, from 40c to 20p, appeared on unwatermarked paper. This was another first, as all previous printings had been on security paper. The lower values of the 1975-76 printings were almost immediately supplanted by the so-called Exporta issue, a new definitive series in current use in Mexico.

Inspection of the Scott listings I have noted will quickly give an idea of the breadth of collecting possibilities. Except for a half-dozen key stamps now cataloging in the low $100s, the rest are well within reach of the average pocketbook. But some of them are very elusive, even though the catalog values are not high. This is especially true of the earlier printings when some of the minor varieties went unnoticed for quite some time.

A fairly complete collection of used stamps should not be too difficult to assemble. The denominations with the largest number of varieties were those that were used most abundantly. This is especially true in regard to colors and shades. The 80c claret, a common airmail

Figure 97. Stamps printed on paper made in Britain appeared later in the series with this watermark.

Figure 98. This 50c stamp with horizontal "MEX-MEX" watermark (British paper) is one of the key stamps of the Architecture and Archaeology series.

Figure 99. These two stamps of 1956 portray men involved in the drafting and passage of the constitution of 1857. The stamps were issued to cover new airmail rates. Although it could be argued that they are commemoratives, they belong to the Architecture and Archaeology definitive series.

Figure 100. This watermark on U.S.-made paper is the last of the three types of watermarks used for the 1950-76 definitives of Mexico.

stamp for many years, was reprinted so many times that a small collection can be made of it alone.

Mounting a collection of these stamps may take some imagination, but there are many perfectly logical possibilities. One could follow the chronological pattern I have outlined here, or the stamps might be arranged by designs or denominations.

If you want to look into this series in more detail, I once again recommend some articles from *Mexicana*.

Light-active varieties on Architecture and Archaeology stamps

Another aspect of these stamps that needs to receive attention is the sequence of late printings on light-active paper. Light-active paper is paper that contains optical brighteners, or that has been coated with light-sensitive material, so that it reacts to ultraviolet light.

For the past 25 years or so, many countries have produced postal paper with these characteristics, both for security reasons and to facilitate high-speed mail handling in rapid-sorting and canceling machines. Mexico is no exception.

In the longwave ultraviolet-light range (3,200-4,000 angstroms), which I have found best for studying Mexican stamps, there are two phenomena of interest: fluorescence and phosphorescence. Both terms refer to behavior of substances under ultraviolet light.

Fluorescence is the result of chemicals called optical brighteners, which are added during the paper-making process. Ordinary fluorescent paper glows, mostly in white to bluish-violet shades, but shows no afterglow when the ultraviolet-light source is removed. Since optical brighteners permeate the paper, fluorescence is normally visible on both the front and back of stamps. "Hi-Brite" is a term often used to refer to a particularly light-active type of this paper.

By contrast, phosphorescence is usually a yellow or amber glow from a surface coating. This glow will persist for a fraction of a second after the ultraviolet-light source is removed.

Mexican postal authorities began experimenting with phosphorescent tagging and fluorescent papers in the late 1960s. It seems there was no public announcement of this, so it took a while for collectors to stumble upon stamps with light-active markings. As a result, collectors who thought they had obtained all stamp varieties discovered they were missing many of those printed on light-active papers.

For example, the photogravure reissues in 1963 of the 80c, 5p, 10p and 20p stamps (Scott C265-C268) were first issued on ordinary papers. However, later printings show both fluorescence and phosphorescent coatings. Since the 80c comes with two die sizes and two different perforation formats, the four Scott-listed stamps actually embrace more than 20 varieties. A few of these are not easy to find.

Figure 101. Some of the experimental airmail coil stamps of 1969, such as the 20c (Scott C347) shown here, were printed on fluorescent paper; others, such as the 80c and 1p shown here, had a phosphorescent coating.

The next airmail stamp series in the Scott catalog (C285-C298) is split about half and half with respect to light-active papers. The engraved 20c, 40c, 50c, 80c and 2p stamps are on slightly fluorescent paper; the photogravure stamps are not. The 40c stamp in this series is quite scarce.

When experimental coil stamps, such as those shown in Figure 101 that first appeared in 1969 (C347-C349), were examined carefully, some were found to have been printed on ordinary fluorescent paper, while others carried a phosphorescent coating on the face of the stamp.

Figure 102. This common denomination 80c airmail stamp (Scott C422) shows, under ultraviolet light, that it was printed on security paper designated for revenue stamps.

In the 1971-73 time frame, there were some printings of several engraved denominations on paper with the vertical "MEX-MEX" watermark (Scott type 300) that looked as though they belonged in the 1955-65 series (Scott C218-C221). On closer inspection, there were three notable differences: The paper had an almost laid appearance; there was blotchy phosphorescence on the face of the stamps when viewed under ultraviolet light; and the perforation holes were smaller than those of the earlier issues.

Scott C422, the 80c airmail stamp, is an interesting variety printed on paper normally reserved for revenue stamps. It shows a beehive pattern of fluorescent lines on either the front or the back of the stamp. This security paper was designated for revenue stamps. An example of the 80c stamp, photographed under UV light, is shown in Figure 102.

The final printings of the Architecture and Archaeology stamps in the mid-1970s, including the two values shown in Figure 103, were all on a chalky-surfaced phosphorescent-coated paper. Some of them (Scott C444-C451) had the "MEX-MEX" watermark; the rest (C471-C480) did not. All but three of these stamps were printed by photogravure, and many were in contemporaneous use with stamps of the then new Exporta series.

Unfortunately, the Scott catalog does not differentiate between the light-active paper varieties, and it should be obvious from this outline that the total picture is quite complex.

The 1982 fifth edition of the catalog of Mexican stamps by Celis Cano contains a table that is very helpful to anyone attempting to search for these varieties. You must understand or translate a few Spanish words and become accustomed to a numbering system entirely different from the Scott listings, but the effort is well-rewarded with a comprehensive picture of what exists.

I know of no album that provides spaces for all these varieties, although the Lighthouse album for Mexico does a good job of annotating and including the major varieties. A showing of the complete series would require mounting on blank pages.

Most of the varieties are still available from dealers specializing in modern Mexican issues, but prices for some have been volatile, and others are beginning to appear on buy lists. I advise you try to complete

Figure 103. Exposed under ultraviolet light, the luminescent coating on the 1975 Architecture and Archaeology airmail issues, including the two stamps shown here, is readily apparent.

your collection before the scarcest of these stamps gets out of reach.

If you are one of those collectors who has not yet experienced the joys of working with ultraviolet light, you really should try it. I feel it will soon be an indispensable tool for collecting modern stamps of almost any country. It can also be most useful in detecting repairs, fugitive hinge marks and filled thins.

If you're in the market for an ultraviolet light, a dual-range ultraviolet light is recommended, with longwave light for Mexican stamps and a shortwave setting for stamps of the United States. Collectors who would like to find out more will do well to refer to *Stamps that Glow* by Wayne L. Youngblood. This is a 96-page booklet published by *Linn's Stamp News*.

Exporta issues

Seventeen years ago, Mexico introduced a new design format for its surface and airmail definitives. They were dubbed the Exporta issues because the stamps depict an array of Mexican products that Mexico desires to promote. Figure 104 shows examples of these stamps. Figure 105 shows examples of the airmail issues.

Specialists predicted early that massive printings required to satisfy postal needs would make the Exporta stamps a prime field for serious collecting and study. This has certainly turned out to be true.

The major difficulty I have had with these stamps is categorizing the varieties. There now are well in excess of 250 major varieties, counting denominations, perforations, paper, watermarks and color shades. If minor color varieties are included, along with the many instances of minor printing flaws (flyspecks), the number probably approaches 500.

While these stamps have been in use, severe inflation in Mexico has rendered some of the early lower denominations virtually useless. Current denominations now range up to 5,000p ($1.60 U.S.).

I owe thanks to many collectors for motivating this introduction to a rather complicated field. Two people have been especially helpful. Wolfgang Schoen of West Germany (staff member of Lighthouse Publications) regularly sends me a detailed listing and catalog cross-reference table his firm prepares to aid collectors in identifying and organizing Exporta stamps. The table appears in a pamphlet titled *Overview of the Exporta Issues*. Lighthouse has a well-constructed

Figure 104. A challenge to collectors because of its complexity, the Exporta issue promotes Mexican products, including steel tubing, cattle and beef, tequila and shoes.

section of album pages for them, which it regularly updates as new varieties appear. The latest supplement covers through 1991.

Enrique Sanchez of Mexico, a self-proclaimed "fanatic" of the Exporta stamps, also sent me a copy of an excellent checklist he had devised to keep track of the various stamps in this series.

What both had in common was that the Exporta stamps should be classified and mounted according to the characteristics of the paper on which they are printed. This is the basis I have used for my study and collecting.

Since Mexican postal authorities rarely have pre-announced issue dates for most of the varieties, it is virtually impossible to organize them in strict chronological order. Separation by paper type will group them in a roughly consistent time sequence. On the other hand, there are numerous varieties of the same denomination (and design), so this may not be a good way to sort them either.

Furthermore, there now are about 26 denominations of surface-mail stamps and 15 different airmails, not all of which exist on the different papers. (Mexico ceased issuing airmail stamps about eight years ago.)

As the name implies, Exporta stamps depict products manufactured or produced within Mexico. These stamps serve as miniature advertising labels on mail leaving the country. The illustrations on the stamps show the standard design. The product occupies the left three-fifths of the stamp, with the export logo, denomination and class of service filling the balance of space. The designs are clean, the stamps are well-printed, and they come in a variety of attractive colors.

In all, 28 subjects, or products, have been featured on Exporta stamps. Continuing inflation in Mexico has caused postage rates to rise sharply, creating a need for stamps with even higher denominations. As a result, many of the product motifs have been recycled one or more times in the stamp designs. New use of an old design has often produced perceptible differences in color, paper or perforation between original stamps and subsequent reprints. There are also several dozen varieties simply as a result of the redenominating of various designs to keep up with Mexico's skyrocketing postal rates. This doesn't even begin to account for the many varieties serious collectors have identified and continue to seek.

During the 17 years that these stamps have been available, assorted papers, with and without light-sensitive coatings, have been used in the many printings. In a few instances, more than one die size exists for a given design. Imperfect control of printing inks has created a number of color shades.

When all these aspects are thrown together, you have a specialist's paradise. As a bonus, there are also some interesting constant plate flaws. Stamps with the cattle and meat design, including the two shown in Figure 106, are typical of the diversity to be found among the Exporta issues. The 80c denomination seen on the left made its debut with the

63

Figure 106. The cattle and meat design from the Exporta series is still in regular use today. The original 80c design is seen at right. A 10p value, issued in December 1987, is shown at far right.

series in the mid-1970s. The five varieties listed in the Scott catalog are among 13 recognized by specialists in these stamps. A later reissue of the cattle and meat design, now in a 10p value, appears on the right.

To bring some order to the 260-plus major varieties now recorded for the Exporta stamps, most specialists divide them into issues. These issues, which follow a rough chronological sequence, are segregated according to the characteristics of the paper on which the stamps are printed. Paper thickness, gum texture and color, and behavior under ultraviolet light are the distinguishing factors.

To be able to make these distinctions, you should possess certain philatelic tools. A paper caliper and a watermark detector are useful. You might be able to get by without the caliper once you get the feel for these stamps, but an ultraviolet light is an absolute necessity. As I stated, a longwave ultraviolet lamp works best with Mexican stamps.

Further key tools for intelligent collecting are catalogs and albums, and here we begin to run into problems. The Scott catalog does not break the Exporta listings into the issue types adequately, and so it is of little use to the specialist. The 1.60p Bicycle airmail stamp is a case in point. The current Scott catalog recognizes the unwatermarked 1975 stamp (Scott C491), a 1981 thin paper variety (Scott C491a) and a watermarked 1979 version (Scott C596). There are actually seven recognizably different varieties of the stamp in the first four issues of the series. Figure 107 depicts the semitransparent paper variety of the third issue 1.60p Bicycle on the left, and a more recent reissue of the design as a 20p surface-mail stamp on the right.

Figure 107. Seven varieties of the 1.60p Bicycle airmail stamp (right) can be recognized by specialists. A new 20p surface-rate value (far right) continues this design in the Exporta series.

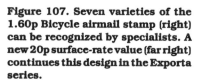

High-value Exportas

On about June 1, 1988, nine new Exporta stamps appeared with face values ranging from 600p to 5,000p. There were no new designs on the stamps, all of which depict Mexican export products that have been previously shown in the Exporta series.

The charts in the appendix on page 103 list the salient characteristics of these and other Exporta stamps. The 600p through 900p denominations appear to be printed on the same paper used for the issue collectors identify as the eighth issue of the Exporta series. The paper is very thick, about 0.10mm. It is unwatermarked, has bright fluorescence on the face (more so than on the gum side of the stamp) and has a dull, somewhat creamy-colored polyvinyl acetate (PVA) gum.

The 1,000p to 5,000p high denominations are printed on entirely different stock, also about 0.10mm thick. The paper is not as white and is what is referred to as granite paper, with randomly embedded fine bluish threads.

The high values are watermarked "MEX-MEX" with the Mexican eagle. This watermark is identified in the Scott catalog as watermark type 300. A tracing is shown as Figure 97 on page 59.

As on previously issued high denominations of the Exporta series, there is a printed burelage or background of fine gray lines that curve to the lower left on the five high values of 1988. The gum is shiny. Under ultraviolet light, the stamps show a low level of splotchy fluorescence.

All of the nine Exporta stamps released in June 1988 are perforated 14. Even though these stamps had a total face value of 18,000p, or roughly $8 at that time, they have proven to be popular with fans of Exporta issues. These stamps feature the highest denominations ever issued by the Mexican post office. Except for the Antonio Caso commemorative of 1983 (Scott 1342), the five high values are Mexico's first extensive use of granite paper.

The five granite paper stamps were designated the ninth issue; the other four fell neatly into the eighth-issue paper category. Of the nine Exporta motifs used, six should be very familiar to collectors, having been prominent in the previous two issues. It was good to see some of the early, less well-known designs brought back.

Figure 108 shows a three-color Jewelry design, last used on the 1981 50p stamp of the fourth issue, now used for the 1988 600p stamp. The 700p stamp shows a strip of film in three colors. This movie film motif was used only once before, on the 1981 20p airmail stamp of the third issue.

The 1,000p Farm Machinery stamp depicts a stylized disc harrow in red and black. The stamp repeats the design of the 5.20p airmail stamp of the 1975-79 first Exporta issue, which hadn't been used on any stamp since then.

Figure 109 shows the 5,000p top denomination of the nine 1988 issues. The stamp shows the cotton boll for its theme. This is the same design selected for the 500p stamps of the seventh and eighth issues. I have to wonder if the strong similarity in designs and denominations may not have caused some confusion among the clerks dispensing stamps at the sales counters. It is true that the green of the 5,000p stamp has more yellow in it than do the 500p stamps, and there is an extra zero in the value. However, at a fast glance, the stamps look much the same. Check the covers you see for accidental overpayment or underfranking.

I obtained a set from each of two different sources and found that one of the 4,000p stamps displayed a brighter fluorescence than the other, but probably not enough to be considered a new variety.

Tenth Exporta series

In the spring of 1989, Guillermo Wilkins of Mexico City sent me a short note, together with a dozen new Exporta stamps. Most of these were varieties I had not yet seen. There were some surprises among them. Ten of the new stamps have characteristics unlike any of their predecessors. The paper of the stamps is fairly thick (approximately 0.11mm), is somewhat opaque and has no watermark. All of the stamps are perforated in gauge 14. Several of the stamps are multicol-

Figure 108. The Exporta Jewelry design of 1983 was revived for use on the 600p denomination issued in June 1988.

Figure 109. This 5,000p Exporta is the highest Mexican denomination ever issued.

Figure 110. Among the most recently introduced Mexican Exporta definitives are two stamps in each of these two designs.

ored. The printed surface is smooth and slightly shiny. The stamps have a matte gum that is off-white, tending toward a cream color.

Some of the stamps, when viewed from the gum side against low-angle incident light, show a pattern of fine parallel lines. When the paper is held up to transmitted light, it might appear to some observers that the paper is a laid variety, but I believe the perception is simply the result of the manner in which the gum was applied, as if with a finely grooved roller. I have learned that this paper was manufactured domestically.

Finally, the stamps exhibit absolutely no ultraviolet-sensitive properties. Under longwave ultraviolet light, the faces of the stamps appear tan in color. The backs of the stamps show a lighter shade.

Four of the stamps in the group share two designs, which are shown in Figure 110. The 700p and 750p stamps depict movie film. They are fairly easy to differentiate. The logo, the numerals of value and one of the film cell colors on the 700p stamp are bluish black in contrast to the 750 issue where the same items are gray. The 900p Piston stamp is printed in black, while its twin, a 950p denomination, is dark blue.

Dealers and collectors refer to this as the tenth series. This issue contains surprises involving the two odd stamps. The 500p Valves stamp shown in Figure 111 is identical to the one in the tenth series in every respect except that its gum is smooth and semiglossy. One dealer assigns this stamp to a new eleventh Exporta issue. Clearly, it does not fit into any of the earlier groups as far as I can tell. Only one other denomination (450p) has surfaced with similar features.

Figure 112 shows the second surprise, a 200p stamp with the citrus fruit design. At first I though it might be a subtle color variety of the 200p tenth-series stamp. On closer examination, it has all the characteristics of the rather limited third-series set. The stamp's thin, semitransparent paper is fluorescent throughout. It has a glossy, dextrin gum. The green color is slightly paler than that of the tenth series stamp. The inscriptions at the foot of the design are less clear. The 200p Citrus stamp also lacks the burelage background of gray curved lines, so there is no risk of confusion with any of the other 200p stamps in the fifth, sixth, seventh or eighth issues.

Another question regarding the Exportas that is repeatedly asked is how to tell the difference between the seventh and eighth issues. They are very similar, and I'm sure many collectors have difficulty with them. For unused copies of these stamps, I have three tests. Compared

Figure 111. Only its gum differentiates this 500p Valves stamp from an earlier Exporta definitive.

Figure 112. This 200p Citrus Fruit design has many characteristics in common with much earlier Exporta stamp issues.

to the seventh issue, the eighth-issue stamps have gum that is less splotchy when viewed against low-angle incident light. They have slightly less intense fluorescence on the face and are slightly more opaque when viewed from the back looking into a light source.

These checks work for me, but I do admit they have not been applied to hundreds of unsorted stamps.

Exporta flyspeck errors

Printing mistakes and flaws always capture the attention of serious collectors. Evidence of this is the philatelic status enjoyed by the U.S. inverted "Jenny" airmail, Scott C3a.

Nothing of that importance is likely to emerge from Mexico's Exporta stamps, but here are some slips that can be fun searching for.

All Exporta stamps carry inscriptions, usually at the bottom or right side of the design, that identify the designer and end in the initials T.I.E.V. (This stands for "Talleres de Impresion de Estampillas y Valores," which translated means the Mexican government printing office for stamps). Hawk-eyed collectors have found numerous instances where the periods following those initials are missing or where there are breaks in some letters. They have determined that the missing periods and broken letters are repetitive and correspond to certain stamp positions on the sheet, which is a characteristic that is essential for calling them constant errors.

Missing periods can be found for the following denominations and issues: 40c (coffee), 1.60p (bicycles), 5p (autos) and 5.20p (farm machinery) of the first issue. In the second, watermarked issue, similar omissions are seen on the 3p, 4p (both designs) and 10p stamps.

Space does not permit a complete rundown of the instances of this happening, but Donald Alexander has described in *Mexicana* the examples he knows about.

Jose Alvarez of Monterrey, Mexico, provided me with several interesting examples of printing flaws that I think are worth looking for. These are somewhat more dramatic. One occurs on the 1.60p Bicycle airmail of the fourth issue. A small orange dot appears at 9 o'clock in the front wheel on stamps in position 48 of panes that bear the registry

Figure 113. One recognized variety of the Exporta issue of Mexico is the 1.60p airmail stamp with an orange spot near the rim of the bicycle wheel.

Figure 114. The broken-pipe variety is evident on the second pipe from the right in the top row on the 6p Exporta stamp. Like other such varieties, it occurs only once in a pane of 50 stamps.

pair numbers. An example of this is shown in Figure 113.

Another printing defect occurs on the 6p Iron Pipe surface-mail stamp. There is a break in the circumference of the pipe in the upper right-hand corner opposite the Exporta insignia. It could be called a broken-pipe variety. It is seen on both the vermilion stamp of the sixth issue and the recent gray stamp of the same design. It occupies position 8 of the pane. An example is shown in Figure 114.

Still another variety is found on the 20p Movie airmail. The stamp in position 36 has a nick at the base of the "0" of the "20." This variety is shown in Figure 115.

Even the more recent printings show some remarkable plate flaws. On varieties of the 450p Electronics stamp issued in 1989 on the paper of issues three (very thin) and 10, there is an inverted "6" on the second "R" of "CORREOS." It occurs in position 40 of every second pane. An example of this variety is shown in Figure 116.

All of these flaws occur only once in a pane, so you may have to examine 100 stamps or so before you find one. But if you do, you will have something at least 50 times scarcer than the normal stamp.

The problems of classifying Exporta stamps still plague the various catalogers. This, in turn, is causing headaches for those people who are designing and printing albums for Mexican stamps. I have heard that Scott probably will revise some of its listings, and that a newly formed committee from MEPSI has offered to assist Scott. Minkus also has produced album pages (and detailed listings) for the many types of Exporta stamps. In any event, the situation is still quite confusing, but several groups are working hard to achieve some order out of the chaos.

Personally, I prefer approaching this challenge with blank album pages and devising a mounting scheme adapted to the material and the theme I wish to develop. It takes a little more time and thought, but will pay dividends in one's understanding and appreciation of the issues.

My basis is the paper type. This is an approach that many of the collectors of classic stamps use with 19th-century issues. It is also a good way to separate stamps on the initial sorting.

Some afterthoughts

The preceding sections are a melding of some of my columns on Exporta stamps. These columns appeared in *Linn's Stamp News* between 1985 and 1989. The stamps continue to be issued in new

Figure 115. A nick can be found in the "0" of "20" on this Exporta airmail stamp.

Figure 116. An inverted "6" is seen over the second "R" of "CORREOS" of this 1989 Exporta stamp.

denominations to cover ever-changing postal rates, although rumors circulate that the series will be replaced with a new definitive issue.

Without catalogs, how can we know what is available in the various issue groupings of the Exporta stamps? A recently updated and expanded checklist of the Exportas appears in the appendix on page 103. I first put this list together several years ago to help me sort out the issues. It is really a composite of information generously supplied from several sources, including collectors and dealers. It contains notes that should enable anyone to determine most of what is present or missing from his Exporta collection.

One difficulty in trying to produce a universal checklist is that the experts can't agree on how many distinct issue groupings there should be. In some cases differences are so subtle that people ignore them. In my list, I have tried to strike a balance that should be acceptable to all but the most picky collectors. My checklist of the Exporta stamps has 11 groupings in all.

It is apt to take some time and practice to become adept at sorting Exporta stamps with the ultraviolet light. The difference between phosphorescence and fluorescence continues to confuse some stamp collectors.

The watermark in the second Exporta issue is usually difficult to see clearly, and I don't have a good solution to that problem. Again, experience is the best teacher. One useful tip with stamps like the Exportas, where minor differences in the character of the paper are important, is to deliberately buy a few sheet-margin stamps. The blank margin selvage gives you an area of paper that is clear of the stamp's design for careful scrutiny.

For those who desire to become serious specialists of the Exportas, I suggest you obtain the earlier mentioned Lighthouse *Mexican Exporta Overview*. Also try to obtain a 1990 specialized price list published by stamp dealer Bill Shelton of San Antonio, Texas. The price list was reprinted in the July 1991 issue of *Mexicana*. Shelton's list is good but contains so much data that some collectors may be overwhelmed. One drawback is that the stamp designs, e.g., steel pipe, movie film, etc., are not described in the listing, making it more difficult to use.

And, of course, another useful source of background information is *Mexicana*. Since the first announcement of these stamps in the April 1976 issue, the editors of *Mexicana* have tried hard to keep up with the series in a quarterly new-issue column. Also, several contributors have written short articles on the Exporta stamps. This is another good reason to join MEPSI if you become addicted to the Exporta stamps.

In summary, the Mexican Exporta stamps are prime candidates for an attractive collection involving some fairly serious philatelic study. Most varieties are still available at modest prices, although there are some scarce ones that require a larger financial commitment. One error, in which the phosphor coating appears on the back of the stamp, is already well into the three-figure range. Fortunately, there are but a handful of varieties in this more expensive category.

Chapter 5

Back of the Book

Provisionals of the post-Maximilian period

If you look near the end of the Scott catalog listings for the stamps of Mexico, you will find a special section devoted to provisional issues. These items, for the most part, constitute some of the aristocrats of Mexican philately.

Provisional stamps of the post-Maximilian period are seldom seen because of their extreme rarity. The only exceptions to this are the provisional stamps issued in the large city of Guadalajara. It takes very deep pockets to collect this material, but it is interesting, nevertheless.

The reasons provisionals exist are not too difficult to explain. As royalist forces began losing their grip on the country, particularly on remote areas that were never strongly held, postmasters were faced with the dilemma of what to do about franking mail. It would be unthinkable to use stamps of the monarchy, even if such were available. Many of the remote offices did not even receive stamp shipments in the last months of French control.

But handling mail without stamps would be cumbersome, too. Still, most postmasters reverted to prestamp franking practices to indicate postage had been prepaid, which was then a postal requirement. This involved reviving the use of old handstamps (sello negro) containing the words "Franca," "Franco," or "Franqueado."

Some offices decided to produce a form of stamps on their own. The postal district of Chiapas was the first to do this, printing a typeset stamp of the design Scott illustrates as A1. This happened in 1866, well before the demise of Maximilian in June 1867. Five denominations were printed on thin paper in light pastel shades. Few of these stamps survive intact because it was customary to affix them to the back of a folded lettersheet across the joint. When the letter was opened, the stamps were destroyed, or at least badly torn. The handful that escaped this fate usually fetch prices very near or above catalog whenever they appear on the market.

Figure 117 shows a canceled Chiapas 1r black-on-light green paper provisional with a Chiapas district overprint on the right.

The provisionals of Cuautla and Cuernavaca were similar to handstamps struck on paper and trimmed to resemble stamps. These were then placed on envelopes or folded lettersheets, as stamps would be, and subsequently canceled.

I have seen a few of the Cuernavaca provisionals. They are not particularly attractive, but a lucky owner does not hesitate to mount only one, either on or off cover, on a single exhibition page.

Figure 117. This used 1866 1r provisional of Chiapas includes the vertical district overprint, seen on the right of the stamp.

Figure 118. These provisional stamps were issued by Guadalajara in 1867. The used 1r stamp (top) is printed on gray-blue paper. The unused 1p (bottom) is on lilac.

The Guadalajara provisionals of 1867 have sufficient varieties (Scott uses 51 numbers to list them) so that a fairly decent collection can be made. And they're not entirely out of reach of the moderately endowed collector. These stamps appear frequently in the stamp market, which is more than you can say for the others. Examples of these provisionals are shown in Figure 118.

I am aware of at least one exhibit-grade collection of the Guadalajara provisionals. Like the Chiapas provisionals, the stamps were mostly printed on thin, colored papers. They were issued either imperforate or with serrate perfs in a circle. Experts have defined several printings, the last of which was in the early months of 1868.

It's worth noting again that, except for 1856-61 remainders used in the capital, Mexico was without a valid issue of stamps from the early summer of 1867 (Maximilian was executed June 19, 1867) until the Hidalgo full-face issue (Scott type A6) appeared on September 8, 1868.

Unfortunately, all 19th-century Mexican provisionals have been extensively counterfeited. This is not surprising since many of them were crude fabrications to begin with and are easy to copy. Luckily, numerous experts have examined this false material, so buyers can expect reasonable protection with certificates of authenticity.

Many years ago, the Scott catalog listed provisionals from Monterey, Morelia and Patzcuaro and provided spaces for them in their specialized Mexico album. They have since been thoroughly studied and declared bogus.

There are two other provisionals in the Scott listing for the 1800s group. The Campeche provisional has long been known and recognized. Again, it is one of those that was handstamped on paper, struck again with a denomination numeral and validated with an initial (rubrica). There were three denominations, and all are rare.

Figure 119 shows a 25c Campeche provisional stamp on an 1876 folded letter to Merida. The oval on the right, struck in gray blue, was a contemporary post office canceler. The oval on the left, struck in blue, was a revenue office handstamp.

The Chihuahua provisional of 1872 has been recognized and listed for only about 25 years.

Prior to the Maximilian era, in 1856, a ½r provisional was issued

Figure 119. The 25c Campeche provisional on this 1876 folded letter to Merida was made by applying oval post office and revenue office handstamps to white paper.

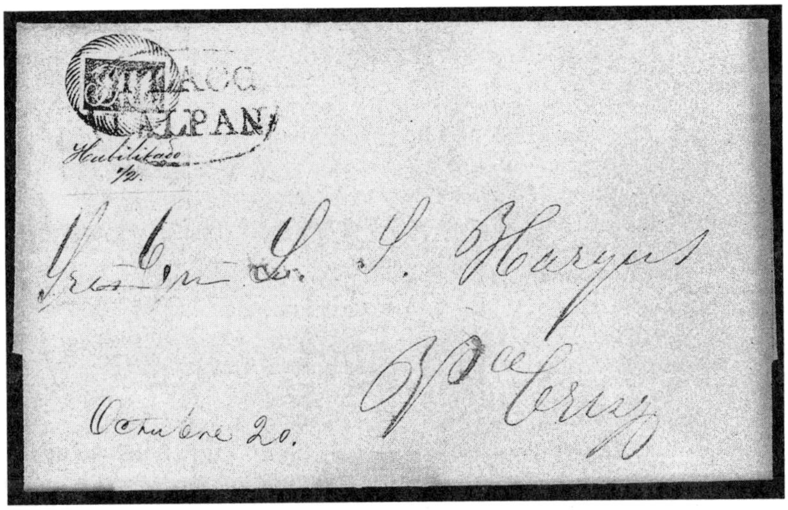

Figure 120. This rare Mexican cover bears the 1856 ½r black Tlacotalpan provisional. It recently sold for $110,000 at a Christie's auction, a record price for a Mexican philatelic item.

for Tlacotalpan, a village in the state of Veracruz. A rare cover bearing the 1856 ½r black Tlacotalpan provisional is shown in Figure 120.

With the exception of a couple of obscure items, this summarizes the major Mexican provisional stamps up to the turn of the century.

Provisionals of the revolution, 1910-16

There is another side to the story of Mexican provisionals, a side that brings us much closer to the present time.

When regular stamps could not be obtained through normal channels or were unavailable because of political upheaval, certain Mexican factions solved the problem by printing their own stamps. This was particularly true during the turbulent years of the revolution, 1910-16. The provisionals of that era are recognized as more than back-of-the-book material. Several Scott-listed regular issues are clearly provisionals, authorized and prepared by temporary or provisional governments. These were not available or not recognized outside local spheres of influence and usually were valid only for brief periods.

These issues, between Scott 321 and 607, appear in many catalogs, but some nevertheless have dubious credentials.

There is no question about the legitimacy of the White and Green Seal issues of Sonora, which were discussed in Chapter 3. These provisionals were used extensively to frank mail. They have been the subject of recent philatelic studies. The same can be said of many of the overprinted varieties of regular engraved Mexican stamps of the 1899 and 1903 series.

However, caution must be used when dealing with the Baja California stamps (Scott 401-404), the "Sonora" and "Plata" overprints, and the Oaxaca stamps (Scott 414-419). To be sure, there are legitimate uses of these stamps, but not so many as the used prices in the catalogs would suggest.

The problem is that stamp collecting was an active hobby at the time of the revolution, and this fact did not escape the parties responsible for stamp issues. Overprint varieties had always been popular with collectors, and there was plenty of material in post office inventories. The distribution of some items was controlled to the extent that certain overprints are much scarcer than others. These scarce items were never made available to the general public and usually reached the stamp market by virtue of inside deals. Scott uses italics

Figure 121. This block of four 10c Sinaloa 1928 provisionals includes two tete-beche pairs. These stamps were never put to use.

to price some of the questionable items.

The Oaxaca provisionals hold a special fascination for collectors of the revolutionary period. They also were discussed in Chapter 3.

Two back-of-the-book listings for provisional issues from Sinaloa (1929) and Yucatan (1924) resulted from momentary uprisings against the entrenched government in Mexico City. At Sinaloa, the Federals regained power so quickly that the provisionals could not even be used. Figure 121 shows a block of four of the 10c Sinaloa provisionals. The block includes two tete-beche pairs.

Yucatan provisionals of 1924 exist imperf and perf 12. There are three denominations. While the stamps are said to have been used locally, few, if any, used copies are to be found. I have never seen any used examples. Figure 122 shows an imperforate block of four of the 5c.

Mexico's provisionals, like other facets of the country's stamps, offer both opportunity and challenge. Few of us can afford the 19th-century provisionals, such as those previously mentioned from Chiapas, Cuautla and Cuernavaca, although those of Guadalajara are more reasonably priced.

While the revolutionary issues are much more accessible, collectors must be wary and do their homework. Fortunately, there is plenty

Figure 122. Yucatan provisionals of 1924 exist imperf and perf 12. There are three denominations. While the stamps are said to have been used locally, few, if any, used copies are to be found.

of reference material. Heed the footnotes in the Scott catalog. Consider acquiring a late edition of the Minkus Latin America catalog; it has more to say about the revolutionary issues than does Scott.

There are rewards for one's efforts. The MEPSI convention at Aripex in Tucson January 23-25, 1987, brought together 100 frames of Mexican material, including four exhibits of the provisionals I've described. Two exhibits dealt with the 1867-68 Guadalajara stamps, and the other two were studies of the Sonora issues. All four exhibits won gold awards.

Revenue collecting

Mexican revenue stamps are plentiful. About twice as many varieties of Mexican revenue stamps exist as there are of all the other kinds of Mexican stamps listed in the regular stamp catalogs. Over the years Mexico derived a large share of its public revenues from the sale of adhesive stamps that certified payment of taxes on all types of commercial activities.

Part of the dilemma faced by would-be collectors is understanding the various classifications of revenue stamps and their purposes. This is essential for a logical and orderly mounting sequence. The Spanish inscriptions on the stamps are not always clear, even if one has a good bilingual dictionary at his elbow. For these reasons, I earnestly advise serious collectors to buy a copy of *The Revenue Stamps of Mexico* by Richard Stevens (1979). It is available from MEPSI. It will help immeasurably in the enjoyment of organizing and mounting a revenue stamp collection.

The first revenue stamps were issued by Mexico in 1874. There were two separate classes or series: Documents and Books (Documentos y Libros) stamps and Federal Tax (Contribucion Federal) stamps.

Here's how they were used: Each businessman or tradesman capitalized in excess of 2,000p was obliged to keep precise business records. Furthermore, he was required to buy and affix revenue stamps, those of the Documents and Books series, to the pages of his account books in proportion to the value of the transactions recorded thereon. An example of a Documentary stamp appears in Figure 123.

The Federal Tax stamps covered a 25-percent surcharge levied by the federal government on all taxable items that towns, cities or states handled. For example, if a merchant had to pay his city 10p for a license to operate his business, he was actually charged 12.50p. The extra 2.50p, for which stamps were affixed to his license, went to the federal government. Regulations governing these taxes were strictly enforced; carelessness resulted in stiff penalties. And the fines imposed were certified by the purchase of even more revenue stamps.

By 1885, two more classes of revenue stamps had been authorized and issued: Custom House taxes (Aduanos) and stamps for taxing commercial transactions (Renta Interior).

As expected, the Custom House stamps were keyed to the value of imports as stated on invoices. The commercial transaction tax was ½ percent, although some of the rates varied depending on the item involved. Imported wines and liquors bore an 8-percent supplemental tax, and similarly higher taxes were paid on tobacco, cigarettes, cigars and snuff.

At the turn of the century, revenue stamps were introduced for other miscellaneous purposes: taxes for the benefit of primary schools, taxes on woven goods and textiles, taxes on the production of precious metals and taxes for the benefit of public health. States and fiscal districts produced and issued their own revenue stamps.

Figure 123. This Documentary stamp comes from the first series issued in 1874. The stamps were produced by the American Bank Note Company in New York City. Note a portion of ABNC's margin inscriptions at upper right of the stamp. The overprinted name in the tablet beneath the portrait varied to indicate place of use. This pen-canceled stamp bears the inscription "Michoacan."

Figure 124. Customs stamps, such as this 10p from the first issue of 1885, were affixed to appropriate documents and then dot-perforated with the name of location of use. This one is punched "FRONTERA."

During the Revolution of 1913-20, General Venustiano Carranza ordered revenue stamps to be printed in the United States. Since the revenue stamps arrived at a time when postage stamps were scarce, they were used temporarily for postage (Scott 347-353). Even the U.S. Armed Forces issued revenue stamps on behalf of Mexico during its occupation of Veracruz in 1914.

From this discussion, one can get a picture of the diversity of revenue stamps available. Each purpose required a different series.

And it didn't stop there. To keep track of receipts in each fiscal year, the designs were changed annually. This is why there are so many varieties. But eventually some of the classifications were modified, and others disappeared altogether.

The early issues were typically in a large format, engraved and very well-printed. Some of these were engraved and printed in the United States and England. The Documents and Books stamps of 1874-75, for example, show a portrait of Miguel Hidalgo y Costilla (as do the first postage stamps) surrounded by elaborate machine engraving. The series consists of 10 denominations in 12 colors. Three paper varieties are known. The stamps were overprinted with the name of the fiscal district in which they were sold and used.

Customs stamps were issued and used at various seaports and entry points where goods were imported. These stamps were perforated with the name of the location where they were used. I suspect they could be considered a form of perfins (stamps punched with perforated initials or designs of holes that stand for letters, numbers or symbols). They came in denominations up to 1,000p, which, in themselves, are not especially scarce. But examples of Custom stamps from the smaller towns where there was little traffic are often quite rare. Figure 124 shows a 10p Customs stamp from the first issue of 1885.

The fact that the designs were changed annually kept the engraving and printing office busy. The early stamps portrayed Mexi-

Figure 125. These two revenue stamps illustrate the types of allegorical motifs typical in the 1930s and '40s. The stamp at far right is overprinted "COMPRA VENTA" (purchases sales), designating its intended use.

can heroes and famous men. By the turn of the century, the designs had shifted to coat-of-arms types and allegorical figures. Stamps became smaller as usage increased and cost of production rose. Figure 125 shows two revenue stamps with allegorical motifs typical in the 1930s and '40s.

But by all standards of comparison, these 19th-century Mexican revenue stamps constitute some of the most elegant philatelic material printed in that era.

At the end of the Revolutionary period (1920), most of the special types of revenue stamps had been discarded. The Internal Revenue (Renta Interior) stamps were being overprinted to indicate the various tax motives for which they were used. This practice continued into the current era. Figure 126 shows one of the early Internal Revenue stamps overprinted and used in Veracruz.

Modern Mexican revenue stamps are mostly of the small size (20mm by 40mm), including talon (a removable part sometimes used for a receipt or control purposes). They exist in a broad array of denominations, colors, overprints and designs. They are eminently collectible and usually not too expensive, even for some that are quite scarce. So, if you're looking for something different, try Mexican revenues. But first, buy the Stevens catalog.

Mexican postage due stamps and usages

Tucked in the back of the Scott catalog listings for Mexico, between the insured-letter issues and the Porte de Mar stamps, are five postage due stamps, Scott J1-J5. These are the only postage due adhesives issued by Mexico. Although it appears that huge numbers were printed, they saw only limited use for their intended purpose.

These stamps have been largely ignored in the standard philatelic literature. I could find very little about them in the references and file clippings I have at hand.

Appearing as they did in 1908, in between the 1903 regular issue and the Independence issue of 1910, it is almost certain they were produced in England by Bradbury, Wilkinson & Company, the same firm that printed the regular issues of that era.

Except for the denomination, the designs of all five stamps are identical. This issue was printed from engraved plates, with an abundance of fine lathe work, a characteristic of stamps of that period. The inscription "TIMBRE" (stamp) appears at the top, flanked by ornate corner ornaments, with "COMPLEMENTARIO" (complementary) in an arc below it. "CORREOS MEXICO" is printed in a wide V pattern beneath the oval that contains the numeral of value. Standard watermarked paper was used (Scott watermark 155). The stamps were perforated in gauge 15.

Figure 127 shows a lightly canceled copy of the 10c high value (Scott J5) of the five-stamp postage due set. Used examples of these stamps are not terribly scarce, but specimens on cover are quite elusive. I leafed through a number of recent auction sale catalogs dealing with mostly Mexican material, and I spotted only a handful of postage dues on cover. Curiously, when cancellation dates were mentioned, most were from 1914, or the early days of the civil uprising in Mexico.

After valuing all five stamps, used and unused, at $2 apiece for some 15 years, the Scott catalog decreased values across the board to $1.25 in 1991, and to $1 in Volume 3 of its 1992 catalog.

Some time ago, while browsing through a prominent cover dealer's stock, I found and borrowed the unusual cover illustrated in

Figure 126. This stamp is from the Internal Revenue series, 1895-96, overprinted and used in Veracruz. It is complete with talon. The stamp shown here was canceled with an oval handstamp, but many revenue stamps were pen-canceled.

Figure 127. A lightly canceled copy of Mexico's 10c postage due stamp.

Figure 128. It shows use of Mexico's postage due stamps on a domestic letter. The city of origin of this cover is unknown (the postmarks are too faint to read), but the 2c Federal stamp from the 1910 issue would normally have paid the rate for a local drop letter. The 2c stamp is perforated with the initials of the addressee, making the cover, in effect, a prepaid business reply envelope. I suspect it was used in Mexico City.

The "No franqueado" handstamp suggests that the Federal stamp was rejected by the local postal authorities, as would have been quite probable if the Constitutionalists were in control of the post office when this letter passed through. A 4c postage due charge was assessed. This is confirmed by the "T" handstamp and the addition of a pair of 2c postage dues. I am convinced that the usage is legitimate and an interesting example of postage due use.

General collectors of Mexico probably encounter postage due stamps for the first time as they attempt to fill the spaces in their albums that are provided for the civil war issues. Beginning in 1914, there are at least six instances when these same postage due stamps — obviously in ample supply — were subjected to various overprints and surcharges to substitute for regular postage stamps. The Scott catalog lists these so-called emergency issues as 381-385, 435-438, 466-470, 495-499, 593-602 and 603-607.

There are plenty of these overprinted varieties available in unused condition, but if you wish to collect them used, beware of favor cancellations. Covers bearing these stamps should be scrutinized carefully, too, to see that cancellations agree with the historical facts of their usage.

Collectors should also be aware that the 1914-15 monogram and "GOBIERNO/$/ CONSTITUCIONALISTA" overprints had mainly to do with validating stamp inventory for whatever rebel force was in control of the post office at the time. Figure 129 shows one such overprint, the Carranza monogram overprint on a 4c postage due, Scott 497. The large Hermosillo "GCM" monogram, the Constitutionalist "$" overprint, and the Villa and the Carranza monograms are all associated with the various rebel movements.

The last two groups of overprints used on these stamps in 1916 are actually surcharges, wherein the face values of the stamps were altered to provide for needed stamp denominations. The reason for this is that during the latter half of 1916, there was such severe monetary deflation in Mexico that postal rates rose sharply to unheard-of levels. For a brief period during November 1916, the postage for a single first-

Figure 128. The perfined 2c stamp on this business envelope was not accepted as valid, possibly because Mexico's post office had changed hands during the chaotic civil wars of the early 20th century. A 4c postage due charge was assessed, paid with a pair of Mexico's 2c postage due stamps.

No franqueado.

Señores

Johannsen, Félix y Cia.

México.

T

Apartado 313.

class letter was $2.50, which probably explains the rationale behind the "GMP/$2.50" surcharges listed as Scott 603-607.

Figure 130 shows the two different types of 1916 surcharges. On the left is a 2c postage due stamp with a 10c violet Barril surcharge (Scott 594), and next to it is a canceled 1c postage due with the "GMP/ $2.50" surcharge (Scott 603). Figure 131 shows the 1p surcharge on the 5c postage due (Scott 601).

Rates soared even higher as the year ended, but the peso was restabilized in early 1917. This ended the need for the civil war overprints. With the return of peace, most of Mexico's manipulated postal paper was declared obsolete, postage had to be paid in hard money and new stamps were soon on the scene (Scott 608-617).

If you enjoy 20th-century postal history, be on the lookout for Mexican postage due covers. An example of one of the surcharged stamps used as regular postage in late 1916 would make a fine addition to anyone's collection.

Figure 129. A 4c postage due with the Carranza overprint.

Figure 130. Among the many surcharged Mexican stamps created in 1916 were this 10c violet Barril surcharge on a 2c postage due (Scott 594) and this canceled copy of the "GMP/$2.50" surcharge on the 1c (Scott 603).

Semipostal and postal tax issues

The only two semipostal stamps issued by Mexico were produced in the waning days of the revolution in 1918. They were intended to raise funds for the Red Cross and are often referred to as the Red Cross overprints. The 5c Hererra and 10c Madero definitives of 1916 were overprinted with a red cross and red surcharges of 3c and 5c, respectively, to create semipostals listed in the Scott catalog as B1-2. Examples are shown in Figure 132.

I do not believe the semipostals saw widespread use. Both mint and used stamps have become fairly scarce in the past 20 years or so.

In the Scott catalog, the postal tax stamp listings for Mexico are tucked between those for the Official stamps and the provisional issues, close to the end of the Mexico section. About 20 major varieties, plus a number of subvarieties, are listed.

The difference between the semipostals and the postal tax stamps is a significant one. The purchase of semipostal stamps was presumably a voluntary action on the part of the mailer. The cost of each individual stamp covered both the postage and the charitable contribution. By contrast, the purchase of postal tax stamps, in most instances, was obligatory. Postal tax stamps were applied independently of the postage stamps that were needed to prepay whatever service the sender desired.

Figure 131. The 1p surcharge on the 5c postage due (Scott 601).

79

Figure 132. Mexico's only semi-postals were issued in 1918 to raise funds for the Red Cross.

All but a few of the Mexican postal tax stamps can be purchased for pennies in either unused or used condition. It isn't too difficult to find them in the stock of dealers who specialize in Mexico. On the other hand, I like covers that demonstrate the correct usage of such stamps. These are not as easy to come by as one might expect. They should be lurking in dealers' boxes of inexpensive 20th-century Mexican covers, but you must know what you are looking for.

The first postal tax stamp, which showed the Morelos Monument, was issued and sold in 1925 to generate funds to fight a locust plague. Among specialists, the postal tax issues are called the locust stamps. There are three Scott-listed varieties, with the unwatermarked stamp being the scarcest of the trio.

Figure 133 shows this stamp used correctly on a cover sent from San Antonio, a small town in Baja California, to San Francisco. This is one of the very few covers that I have seen bearing the first postal tax stamp. I suspect the obligatory use of these stamps was often overlooked by post office clerks.

When the locust campaign ended in the early 1930s, the surplus stamps were put to postal use paying the rate for intracity drop letters and circulars. This is noted in the Scott catalog footnote following the

Figure 133. A 1c postal tax stamp and a 10c postage stamp of similar design on a 1925 Mexican cover to San Francisco.

Figure 134. Two Mexican Mother
and Child postal tax stamps of 1929,
Scott RA6-7.

listing for 687A. Pay careful heed to the gauge of perforation on used
copies of the stamp. If it is perforated in gauge 12, the stamp was used
to pay postal tax. If it is perf 10½, it was probably used for postage. The
use of this stamp is often misidentified in dealer stock books and club
circuit books.

The next group of postal tax stamps raised money for child
welfare, particularly the support of orphans. Initially, the drive for
funds was launched with the Morelos Monument stamp vertically
overprinted in red with the words "Proteccion Infancia." As the Scott
catalog notes, there were two settings of this overprint, both of which
are equally abundant. This stamp with the overprint reading down
instead of up is considerably scarcer, but beware of forgeries.

Figure 134 shows two of the Mother and Child postal tax stamp
designs issued in 1929. The lithographed stamps have a number of
interesting variations, none of which is particularly scarce. It would be
quite a challenge to find them all properly used on cover. Figure 135
shows one such cover bearing Scott RA5. I located it in a dealer's
bargain cover box. If you are looking for completeness, try to find the
booklet panes and imperforate varieties of these issues as well.

In 1930 the 2c and 5c Mother and Child postal tax stamps were
revalued to 1c with an "HABILITADO/$0.01" surcharge. With a world

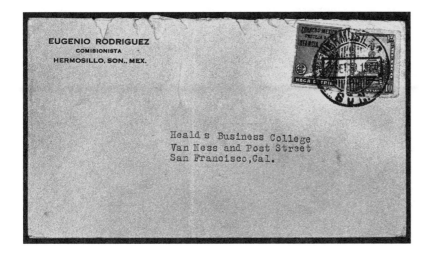

Figure 135. The first Mother and
Child postal tax stamp is tied next
to a 10c definitive on a 1930 cover
from Hermosillo to California.

Figure 136. Mexico relied upon postal tax stamps to help fund the fight against malaria in 1939 (top) and a drive to promote literacy in 1946-47 (bottom).

financial crisis then in full swing, there probably wasn't much demand for higher values.

In 1931 remainders of an overprinted revolutionary-era stamp, Scott 423, were given an added "PRO INFANCI" overprint in red. These are listed as Scott RA13. This was the last postal tax stamp issued to support the children's welfare fund. I have yet to find one on cover.

A special stamp was issued in 1939 to finance a drive to eradicate malaria in Mexico. As shown at top in Figure 136, the design of the stamp was most striking—a monstrous mosquito preying upon a man with outstretched arms. Once again the use of these stamps was obligatory. Examples on covers from the World War II period are plentiful. This stamp exists with three different watermarks and also can be found imperforate. It is probably the most common of all of Mexico's postal tax stamps.

Rounding out the short list of Mexican postal tax stamps are a 1c bright red Miguel Hidalgo stamp issued in 1941 and a 1c Pro-Literacy stamp that appeared in 1946. A used copy of the Pro-Literacy stamp is shown at bottom in Figure 136.

The Hidalgo stamp was sold to support restoration work in Dolores Hidalgo, the city where Father Hidalgo launched the Mexican independence movement in 1810. Figure 137 shows a contemporary use of this stamp on cover. The 1946 Pro-Literacy postal tax stamp, showing hands removing a blindfold and pointing to an alphabet chart, was a companion to the set of regular and airmail (Scott 806-11 and C153-57) stamps issued in 1945 to publicize the national literacy campaign in Mexico.

The 1947 printing of the Pro-Literacy stamp on "GOBIERNO MEXICANO" and eagle in circle fiscal-watermarked paper (Scott RA18) is probably the scarcest variety of any postal tax stamp. It is difficult to find in mint condition.

For the thrill of the hunt in modern Mexican postal history, the next time you are thumbing through cheap foreign covers at a dealers' bourse, see if you can find some postal tax stamp usages. They are good items to add to your collection of Mexico.

Tuberculosis seals

Mexico was late among world nations joining the battle against the ravages of TB. A national committee was not organized until 1940. The committee quickly adopted a proven fund-raising method, and in

Figure 137. The 1c Hidalgo postal tax stamp on this 1941 airmail cover supported restoration work in the Mexican city of Dolores Hidalgo.

Figure 138. Mexico's first tuberculosis seals of 1943 were produced in both a scarce single-frameline variety (far left) and the more common double-frameline variety (left).

1943 the first TB seals were put on sale to the public.

Figure 138 shows Mexico's first TB seals, which exist in two types. The seal on the left has a single outer frameline around the design. The seal on the right, a much more common type, has a double frameline.

Whereas TB seals of the United States and most other countries were printed by private firms, Mexican seals were produced in the government printing office, the same institution responsible for postage stamps and other government paper. In addition, the seals were printed on the same watermarked postal paper used for contemporary postage stamps. This practice continued until 1954. These early Mexican seals can be found with three different watermarks, listed in the Scott catalog as types 272, 279 and 300.

With the exception of the first two issues, all Mexican TB seals were denominated and were sold primarily at post offices. A single stamp design was used each year from 1943 through 1955, which was the first year TB seals were printed by a private contractor. Figure 139 shows a cover with the 1955 seal tied to the left of a 25c airmail stamp.

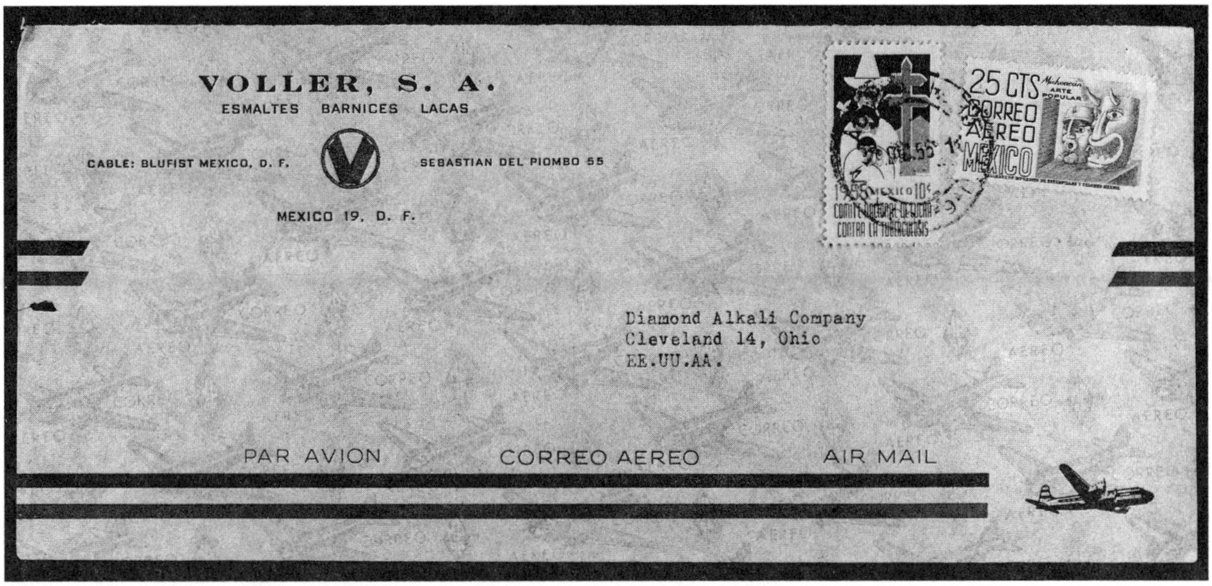

Figure 139. A Mexican TB seal of 1955 is well tied to this commercial airmail cover.

Figure 140. The 1948 TB seal on the left was produced by the same government printing office that printed the Mexican airmail stamp on the right, both from a 1950 cover to New York.

Curiously, for the years 1949 and 1950 Mexico used surplus 1948 seals with special revalidation overprints. Five different types of these overprints have been recorded. Figure 140 shows two stamps photographically cropped from a commercial airmail cover to New York. Though mailed to New York in 1950, this cover shows a curious usage of an unoverprinted 1948 TB seal. The barely visible inscription just below the design of both the airmail stamp and the TB seal reads: "TALLERES DE IMP(RESSION) DE EST(AMPILLAS) Y VALORES MEXICO." With that inscription marking this adhesive as printed by the government, and a "5c" denomination shown, is it any wonder some collectors treat Mexico's TB seals as stamps?

The design theme of the early seals was clearly focused on the eradication of tuberculosis. During the last three decades, many of the seals have been devoid of designs or inscriptions relating to health matters except for the familiar double-barred cross, the international symbol for TB agencies.

Commencing in 1956, Mexico's TB seals were printed in sheets with multiple designs, the first displaying 50 different Christmas motifs. Since then, more than 1,000 distinct designs have been used, including tropical fish, butterflies, monuments, churches, military uniforms, popular art, regional costumes and so forth.

Figure 141 shows three seals of the 1960s, conveying some idea of this range of subject matter. If these were bona-fide postage stamps, they would be a gold mine for topicalists. Figure 142 shows more stamps from the 1960s, issued for the Comite National de Lucha Contra la Tuberculosis (National Committee in the Fight Against Tuberculosis).

Over the years, the face value of the TB seals has increased steadily. It was 5c in the beginning, from 1945 to 1952. It was then raised to 10c and remained there until 1977, when it doubled once more to 20c. In 1984-85, when Mexico's currency devaluation became severe, the price for seals was pegged at 1p. It rose to 2p in 1986, took a fivefold jump to 10p in 1987, and then doubled to 20p for 1988-89.

The official philatelic status of these TB seals is not clear. There have been several instances of the use of a postal tax in Mexico to generate funds for special causes. A locust plague, child welfare and malaria eradication through mosquito control were all supported by the obligatory use of special tax stamps on the mail, as discussed earlier in this chapter. But I have been unable to find evidence to indicate that this has ever been the case with the TB seals. However,

Figure 141. Starting in the 1960s, the emphasis on health came to be replaced by a wealth of colorful topics on Mexico's TB seals.

Figure 142. More Mexican TB stamps from the 1960s.

we know seals are sold aggressively by the Mexican postal service, which for years constituted the seals' major retail outlet.

A.W. Bork is a life member of MEPSI and a onetime resident of Mexico. He has observed that post office window customers were often the subject of mild coercion by the clerks to take their change in TB seals and use the seals in addition to the regular postage on letters presented for mailing. This was especially true during the Christmas holiday season when the seals were actively promoted. Bork also notes that unsuspecting tourists have used the seals in the belief that they were valid for postage, since they were purchased at the post office window and they display denominations.

In any case, TB seals are used extensively on mail during the holidays and often receive cancels just like regular stamps. Finding covers bearing them is not difficult.

Are Mexican TB seals collectible? Apparently so, because there is a small but avid group that takes them quite seriously. Most of the seals are available for pennies. Even full sheets of the multiple design issues are traded for just a few dollars.

The early issues printed by the Mexican government are getting more difficult to find. The 1945 stamp is especially scarce, now selling for well above $10 a copy. The only other pricey items are the 1943 stamp with single frameline, the 1950 issue, a 1948 remainder with the "campana/1950" (campaign/1950) overprint, and a 1975 souvenir sheet featuring the Cathedral of Mexico City. The souvenir sheet sold for $80 U.S. when issued.

In 1972, MEPSI published a short monograph by Henry Irwin titled *The Tuberculosis Seals of Mexico*. As far as I know, it is still available. Irwin obtained some of his information from the out-of-print, but still available *Green's Catalog of the Tuberculosis Seals of the World*, originally compiled by Dick Green.

Chapter 6

Postal History

Collecting Mexican cancellations

One of the remarkable things about Mexican philately is the number of diverse aspects that can be the subject of serious study and/or a first-rate collection. A few years ago I had the opportunity to examine a fairly large holding of stampless covers. It was the source of considerable excitement because there is always the chance of seeing some postal markings for the first time. And such was the case here.

Mexico offers some interesting, if not unique opportunities in the area of stampless covers. Until the introduction of stamps in 1856, all domestic and outbound foreign mail moved as stampless letters. As most of us know, the idea behind postage stamps was a means for prepaying postage fees. Prior to that time, nearly all mail was sent collect, with the addressee being responsible for postage.

The earliest stampless letters known from Mexico date from the Spanish colonial era. That would be before 1820 and going back to the late 1700s. The Spanish had established a fairly good mail system in their colonies of the Western Hemisphere. Their methods were adopted by most of the independent countries that later came into being.

Marking devices were used to indicate the origin of letters. These quaint and attractive town marks are much sought after by collectors. Postage rates, usually following some obscure tariff, were marked on the letters in manuscript most of the time. In some instances, letters dealing with official government business were sent free of postage and so marked. This could be considered a form of free franking. All covers from the colonial period are scarce, and most are beyond the means of the average collector.

When the War for Independence ended in 1820, Mexico entered what most historians call the Republic period. Until stamps appeared, mail continued to be handled in a manner similar to that prevailing in colonial times. Handstamps, many of which were the same ones the Spanish used, marked the names of towns where the mail was dispatched.

As business and commerce expanded, so did the postal system. This meant there were more towns of enough importance to have post offices, so the list of collectible town marks grew correspondingly. Since there seemed to be no set standards as to the form of these postmarks, they came in all shapes and sizes, which further endears them to collectors. In addition to the common straightline names, there exist boxes, ovals, fancy wreaths, ribbons and numerous other ornate, handcarved designs. Some are quite common; others are scarce.

Figure 143. San Felipe del Obraje was originally a separate district office but later became a suboffice of Maravatio. This cancellation, pictured in the Schatzkes Mexican cancellation book, is found only on the stamps of 1856 and is one of the rarest markings known.

Handstamped numerals were used more and more to indicate the amount of postage to be collected. Prepayment of postage was still the exception, but in those cases where it took place, the larger post offices usually had supplementary handstamps containing the words "Franco," "Franca" or "Franqueado" to indicate postage had been paid.

During the first months of the stamp period, beginning in August 1856, letters could go either paid or unpaid. To encourage prepayment, the rates for unpaid letters were higher. Still, a few people sent letters collect, especially if they had reason to suspect the mails might not get through because of the ever-present highway bandits.

Figures 143 and 144 show examples of markings used in 1856. One of the rarest markings known is the San Felipe del Obraje marking shown in Figure 143. Figure 144 shows a cancellation used in the district of Toluca by the stagecoach (diligencia) line that carried the mail between Toluca and Mexico City in 1856.

The introduction of stamps did not end the stream of Mexican stampless letters. Even after stamps were issued, there were many instances where small or remote offices did not receive stamps. So they simply used the pre-stamp franking methods they knew so well. Once in a while such letters were marked with an explanation: "No hay estampillas," Spanish for "there are no stamps." Figure 145 shows an example of this.

At other times during the turbulent years following the introduction of stamps, mail was routinely carried without them. For example, during the waning years of the Maximilian period (1864-67), postal agents in the cities and towns controlled by the Republican forces under Benito Juarez refused or were forbidden to use the current issue of stamps bearing the likeness of Maximilian. Old "Franco" handstamps were brought out and used to indicate postage had been paid (prepayment was still obligatory).

As mentioned previously, postal historians refer to this type of usage as "sello negro." Sello negro covers from this period are fairly common, especially from the cities that were never strongly held by the monarchists.

Another period from which stampless covers are occasionally seen was 1871 to 1872, when the Mexicans were having trouble with postal forgeries and the new 1872 issue was late. Figure 146 shows an example of this practice.

Finally, most foreign-bound Mexican mail was sent stampless until 1879, when Mexico joined the Universal Postal Union. Only then could letters be sent completely prepaid with postage stamps to other member countries of the UPU. Until Mexico joined the UPU, some letters left Mexico with stamps. The stamps paid the domestic portion of the postage.

Covers exist with combination usage: Mexican stamps paying the internal rate and British stamps, for example, paying the sea rate to England or some port on the continent. But these usages are quite scarce, and very expensive. Still, a representative collection of Mexican stampless covers can be assembled within the budgets of most serious collectors. Large correspondences from the 1830s to the 1860s have survived and provide the philatelic market with stampless material. Generally, stampless covers, except those from small, scarce districts and towns, are much cheaper than those with stamps. That doesn't make them any less desirable or less interesting from a philatelic standpoint. The abundance of attractive designs and forms, combined with the various colors in which they can be found, are further lures to the collector.

Figure 144. This cancellation, also pictured in the Schatzkes book, was used in the district of Toluca, 65 kilometers west of Mexico City, by the stagecoach (diligencia) line that carried mail between the two cities in 1856.

Figure 145. A small fragment of a cover on which a postal agent in Candela, a small village in the postal district of Saltillo, used the "Franco" handstamp with the handwritten explanation, "There are no stamps." The handstamp is dated November 24, 1857.

Figure 146. A late sello negro usage on a circular-rated (½r) business announcement. It is dated February 3, 1871, and originated at Minatitlan, a town on the eastern edge of the state of Veracruz.

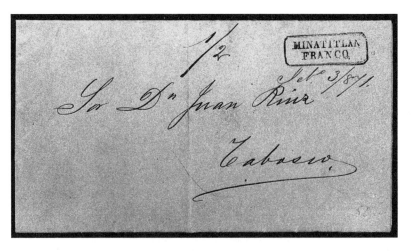

Figure 147. The 1884-85 stamp pictured at the top is canceled by a Cholula handstamp dating to circa 1780. The handstamp is shown below the stamp.

Some postmarks sustained a long period of use. They can be found used on colonial pieces, on letters from the pre-stamp era, and right up into the stamp period. A small town in the postal district of Puebla, for example, used a device to cancel stamps more than 100 years after its first recorded use on a Spanish colonial letter. This Cholula handstamp is shown in Figure 147. There are other marks with extended usage if you enjoy searching for them (and I do!).

Stampless foreign covers from Mexico aren't terribly difficult to find, and some aren't too expensive either. Normally these items also will have other postmarks on them, from the United States, Great Britain, France, and so on. Determining the routing and rate structure on these covers can sometimes turn into a pleasant evening of research (assuming you have or can get to basic references).

A few words of advice if you decide to collect stampless covers: Do spend some time with two basic reference books: *The Pre-Stamp Postal Markings of Mexico* by Otto Yag and John Bash, published by MEPSI in 1965 and updated in 1971, and *The Cancellations of Mexico* by Joseph Schatzkes and revised by Karl H. Schimmer in 1983 and published by W.E. Shelton. The second book is still in print, and both items are available on loan to American Philatelic Society members from the American Philatelic Research Library.

Although I know of no attempts to forge or counterfeit Mexican stampless covers, watch for attempts to alter or enhance scarce markings. Try to secure the best possible strikes of common markings. You may have to compromise a bit on the scarce to rare ones, but I have seen many medium to poor grade stampless covers being pushed by dealers or at auction.

Foreign-bound mail prior to the UPU

Postal history buffs of the Caribbean area will readily recognize the names of two ports on the Gulf of Mexico: Tampico and Veracruz. These two Mexican cities were important outlets for Mexican produce during the 19th century and also were focal points for increasing European business interests.

When Great Britain established diplomatic relations with Mexico in 1825 (following the ouster of Spanish rulers), it set up a postal agency in the consulate at Veracruz. The British legation in Mexico City also kept in frequent contact. Since these two offices were looking after the interests of British subjects doing business in Mexico, it was only natural that they developed fast and efficient freight and mail connec-

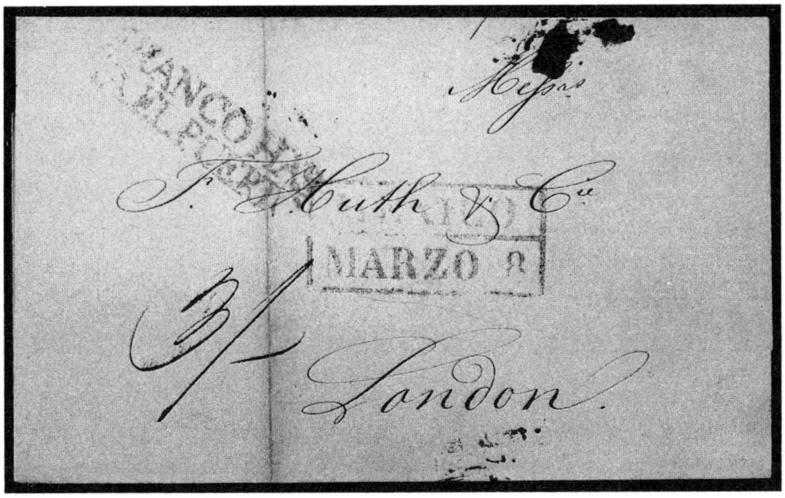

Figure 148. Placed into the Mexican mails at Mexico City on March 8, 1835, this letter was prepaid as far as Veracruz, as noted by the "Hasta el Puerto" handstamp. It reached London via British packet, where the addressee paid an additional 3 shillings for delivery.

tions to London, Europe and many Caribbean ports. Anyone was welcome to use the mail service.

One of the earliest Mexican postal markings associated with the British conveyance opportunity was a double straightline "FRANCA HAS/TA EL PUERTO," which meant: Postage paid to the port. Letters deposited in the Mexican mails addressed to foreign destinations could be prepaid as far as the Mexican port of departure and no further.

A letter mailed in Mexico City, for example, would be carried by the courier of the British legation to Veracruz and put aboard a British ship there by the postal agent. It would then go forward by British packet toward its final destination.

Shown as Figure 148 is a cover bearing these markings. Placed into the Mexican mails at Mexico City on March 8, 1835, the letter was prepaid as far as Veracruz, as noted by the "Hasta el Puerto" handstamp. It reached London via British packet, where the addressee paid an additional 3 shillings for delivery.

As British interests grew, a similar agency was established at the consulate in Tampico in the early 1840s. This coincided with the formation of the Royal Mail Steam Packet Company, which provided direct connections from both Tampico and Veracruz to Southampton via Havana, Nassau and St. Thomas.

As a result of all this, the British formed a virtual monopoly on foreign-bound mail originating in Mexico. Thousands of letters were deposited with one or the other of these offices for handling. And the handling was, as we would expect, efficiently carried out.

Both Mexican offices had their own distinctive handstamp devices used in processing mail. What we call consular post office datestamps consisted of a double-ring handstamp with the name of the office forming the top arc of the circle. This format was roughly the same for all British foreign offices.

In addition to these datestamps, there were "Paid" stamps consisting of a crown at the top of a circle containing the words "Paid at (name of city)." These "crowned circles" were issued to numerous British outposts in the Americas and are highly prized by collectors. Mail passing through these offices received appropriate markings. All received datestamps. Some received paid markings, rate marks and routings if appropriate. Transit marks were applied on the way.

Even though the two offices presumably operated under the same

Figure 149. This Veracruz British consular post office marking is on the reverse of an 1846 letter from Mexico to London.

Figure 150. Crowned-circle paid markings were applied in red ink at Tampico and in black ink at Veracruz.

Figure 151. The "C63" marking saw extensive use canceling British stamps at Tampico during the late 1860s and early 1870s. The "C64" marking is not known to have been used by Veracruz postal agents.

Figure 152. This piece has a 4-penny British stamp that was used and canceled at Tampico with the "C63" handstamp. It was destined for Veracruz and probably went via the Royal Mail Steam Company. The approximate date is 1870.

rules, there are curious differences between them. The folks at Tampico usually used red ink for their handstamps, while the agents at Veracruz preferred black ink. If there was a reason for this, I am unaware of it.

Consular post office datestamps are not difficult to find on foreign letters from Mexico, and they are not very expensive. An example of a Veracruz British consular postmark is shown in Figure 149. The crowned-circle paid markings are another matter. They are quite scarce, especially from Tampico. Good strikes often fetch hundreds of dollars, depending on what else is on the letter. Their scarcity stems partly from the fact that during the period they were used, most letters were sent unpaid or collect. Figure 150 shows tracings of crowned-circle paid markings.

Since the packets steamed both north and south between Tampico and Veracruz, Mexicans frequently availed themselves of the mail service between the two ports instead of sending letters overland. They did this despite the 1/- packet fee in addition to the 2r they paid for domestic postage. Perhaps the speed and safety were worth it.

During the French invasion of 1862 and the subsequent short reign of Maximilian, responsibility for all civilian mail remained with the Mexican post office, and French and British packet steamers continued to be used freely for overseas mail.

In about 1865, British stamps came to Mexico to be used in the consular post offices on prepaid mail handled by them. At the same time, "C" type cancelers were issued to the offices to use on the stamps. Tracings of "C63" and "C64" markings are shown in Figure 151. Veracruz was recorded as having been assigned canceler "C64" but was never issued stamps nor, as far as I know, the canceler.

The "C63" handstamp was issued to Tampico, and here the story is quite different. Numerous examples of its use have been recorded. During the late 1860s and early 1870s, we find many examples of letters that were sent from Tampico to Veracruz (and points inland) with attractive combinations of both British and Mexican stamps. British stamps paid the packet fees; the Mexican stamps covered inland postage. One such example is shown in Figure 152.

British consular post offices began to decline during the 1870s, and they were finally closed in 1876. They had served well for nearly 50 years, but viable alternatives for transferring mail abroad appeared. The Universal Postal Union was being formed to simplify exchange of mail between countries, and Mexico joined in 1879.

French army post office in Mexico

Chapter 1 dealt with the postage stamps used in Mexico during the brief monarchy of Archduke Maximilian, 1864-67. Throughout that period, Maximilian was supported by a substantial army of French soldiers, including small contingents of Belgians and Austrians.

French military presence in Mexico actually began two years before Maximilian and Carlota stepped ashore at Veracruz on June 12, 1864. Originally, the French had been joined by British and Spanish units to force collections of a large foreign debt that Mexicans had refused to repay on time. When it became evident that the French had designs on extending their empire into the Western Hemisphere with the debt-collection pretext, England and Spain quickly withdrew their forces.

To facilitate communication between dispersed units of the army and to expedite mail from the military back home, the French established post offices in the major cities under their control, as well as in

Figure 153. Postmarks applied by French army field post offices.

certain other field locations. These were called bureaus. Each bureau was supplied with contemporary French stamps together with appropriate datestamps and canceling devices. Figure 153 shows postmarks applied by French army field post offices. This was really a mail system within a mail system, since the Mexican post office also was operating at the time.

The identification of letters that were handled in this system is not difficult, although finding the letters is difficult. They nearly always bear a double-ring datestamp inscribed "Corps Exp Mexique," which stands for Mexican Expeditionary Force. At the base of the handstamp is "Bau" plus a letter, which designates the bureau or post office at which the letter was mailed. There were 12 bureaus, each identified by a letter. "A" was the bureau situated at Mexico City. "B," "C" and "D" designated French army headquarters at Veracruz, and so on.

Killers used to cancel the stamps consisted of a rhomboid of dots. There were eight rows of dots each way, with four initials in the center of the rhomboid. Again, the initials tell us where the letter originated. The first three, always "CEM," stand for Corps Expeditionaire Mexique. The fourth letter, as noted, signifies the bureau where it was used.

The French stamps used on these letters were from the two issues of the so-called Napoleon Head Empires, either imperforate or perforated (Scott 12-28). Postal rates were such that the denominations used were mostly the 10 centimes, 20c and 40c. All examples of mail of this type that I have seen were directed to places outside of Mexico, usually to France. I know of one cover that went to Algeria.

Unfortunately, Corps Mexique covers are scarce and fetch high prices in the stamp market. There also were stampless letters, and these usually trade for somewhat less than covers with stamps.

Once in a while a loose stamp is found with the "CEM" and letter

Figure 154. This January 9, 1866, cover is from the French army post office in Mexico City. It was sent to Bordeaux, France, where it arrived February 6. The datestamp shows the words, "Corps Exp Mexique" and the letter "A." The killer is a rhomboid of dots with the letters "CEMA." The "A" identifies the Mexico City office.

Figure 155. Rare postmarks used on French (left) and British (center and right) troop transports.

initials, but I suspect that by now most of them have been picked out of everyone's bulk stock. The "CEMA" covers mailed at Mexico City are by far the most plentiful. One of these is illustrated in Figure 154. Next come those from Veracruz, with "CEMB" or "CEMC." When you get to the lower ranking letters like "H," "K" and "M," which were assigned to the smaller bureaus, they are true rarities.

Another thing that enhances the desirability and demand for Corps Mexique covers is their suitability for many different types of collections or exhibits. They will fit nicely in a collection of classic Mexican postal history or in a collection of French classics and offices abroad. And since most of the letters bear additional transit and ship markings, they are ideal for a collection or exhibit of maritime mail. Figure 155 shows rare postmarks used on troop transports.

I realize that not too many of us can aspire to own many such covers, but I have always been fascinated with this small segment of Mexican postal history. It makes a good story, too.

Postmaster General Cosme Hinojosa

Unless you happen to be a keen student of the civil war stamps of Mexico, the name Cosme Hinojosa will probably mean nothing to you. But he, perhaps more than any other individual or factor, was responsible for the bewildering array of Mexican stamp varieties issued between 1913 and 1917.

As a native of the state of Sonora, Hinojosa became involved politically in the early stirrings of the revolutionary movement in northern Mexico. He was elected to the state legislature in 1910.

In 1913 he was named director general of the posts by Venustiano Carranza, who had formed a revolutionary cabinet in Hermosillo in opposition to the federal government in Mexico City. They called themselves the constitutionalists. For Hinojosa, it was the beginning of a long tenure as one of the top postal officials of Mexico. In the tumultuous years that followed, he developed the uncanny knack for picking the right side to be on among the various warring factions.

When Carranza finally established himself as chief of the central government in Mexico City, Hinojosa became the postmaster general, a position he held continuously until 1928. It was even before he attained this post that he discovered the potential of selling postage stamps to collectors, who were always on the lookout for new varieties. Hinojosa was also keenly aware of the possibilities of personal gain in providing those varieties.

As director general of posts in Sonora, he authorized nearly all of the local issues of that era. These included the White Seal and Green Seal provisionals (Scott 321-346), which were discussed in Chapter 3; the temporary use of revenue stamps for postage (Scott 347-353); and the various transitory issues (Scott 354-361).

Hinojosa was also behind the order of samples from George Linn of the perforated 5c Transitorio stamp. Figure 156 shows the stamp,

Scott 369. A printer before he was a philatelic publisher, Linn shipped some 75,000 copies of the stamp, expecting payment since they were eventually put to use. But not only did Hinojosa's department refuse to pay, it later disavowed as counterfeits those stamps that had seen postal service!

The reason for these local and provisional stamps is easily explained. When the constitutionalists seized control of the federal offices in Sonora, nearly all the federal postmasters fled the region, mostly to the safety of border towns in the United States, taking their stamps with them. What few stamps remained were woefully inadequate for postal needs.

Carranza's army marched south and took control of the capital. Hinojosa took the top job of director general of posts in the central post office. There he issued several decrees authorizing use of various monogram overprints to validate stocks of stamps found in the vaults, mostly the 1910 Centenary issue. This overprinting assured that postal revenues would accrue to the government then in control, since the federals had carried off quantities of stamped paper when they were driven from the city.

For a brief time in late 1914, Carranza and his followers were forced from the capital by the agrarian reformer, Emiliano Zapata. Hinojosa transferred his operations to Veracruz. When the short-lived alliance between Zapata and Pancho Villa collapsed, during which time the so-called Villa overprints appeared, the constitutionalists returned to Mexico City. Hinojosa brought with him a fresh supply of 1910 stamps, which had just been received from the printer in England. With this ample supply of raw material at hand, the frantic overprinting resumed. Facsimiles of the overprints used during this period can be seen in the Mexico listings in the Scott catalog for the years 1914 to 1916. Nearly all of the overprints can be ascribed to Hinojosa's authority.

Figure 157 shows three of the overprints to good effect as they appear on 1910 Independence issue stamps. From left to right, the stamps show the 1914 dollar-sign overprint of the constitutionalist government (Scott 426), the 1915 Carranza monogram overprint (Scott 489) and the 1916 "Barril" or barrel surcharge (Scott 580).

There is no question that many overprint varieties were produced for the express purpose of boosting sales to collectors and dealers. Hinojosa saw to it that some of them were intentionally printed in very limited quantities so they might command higher prices. He even traveled to the United States in 1915 to sell Mexican stamps. He brought remainder stocks of many of the war issues, including the Sonora locals, and the small printings of the overprinted 1899-1903 issues, plus high denominations that were particularly sought after.

Hinojosa often told a dealer he was selling his entire holding of certain remainders to him (at large multiples of face value, of course). Then he would move on to the next dealer, with the same story.

Hinojosa made a similar selling trip in 1916. In the meantime, he had formed an alliance with Javier J. Favela, proprietor of Bolsa Filatelica de Mexico (the Mexican Stamp Exchange). This, in effect, became Hinojosa's largest retail outlet.

This maneuver did not sit well with Hinojosa's U.S. customers. Most honest collectors and dealers had nothing but disdain for his actions. In the span of just a few short years, Hinojosa had besmirched the philatelic reputation of what had been considered a relatively reliable stamp-issuing nation.

It is perhaps unfortunate that Scott chose to list so many of

Figure 156. When he was director general of posts in Sonora, Cosme Hinojosa procured and used (but never paid for) 75,000 copies of this stamp, Scott 369. The agrieved creditor was none other than George W. Linn, who later founded *Linn's Stamp News*.

Figure 157. A few of the 1913-17 Mexican overprints that owe their existence to Cosme Hinojosa. Shown from left to right are the dollar-sign overprint, Carranza monogram and Barril surcharge.

Hinojosa's contrived issues in the normal numbering sequence in its catalog. While all the stamps listed could have been used for postage, most of the scarce varieties were never offered for sale to the public, and few were ever used.

Nick Follansbee, one of the contemporary experts in the Mexican revolutionary era, has written extensively about these stamps in *Mexicana*. Follansbee prefers to call the stamps the "Hinojosa special printings." He warns collectors to be wary of the many counterfeit overprints that exist, particularly in the short printings.

Hinojosa himself wrote a short book in English on the 1913-17 revolutionary stamps. It makes absolutely no mention of the scarce varieties for which he was responsible, but does contain excellent translations of the various decrees dealing with the issues. This makes the book quite interesting and useful.

Wells, Fargo mail service

For most people, the name Wells, Fargo conjures up visions of stagecoaches lumbering over dusty Western roads and trails, or perhaps the express and banking operations for which Wells, Fargo became so famous. This section will describe the activities of Wells, Fargo in the handling of mail and small packages in Mexico during the last two decades of the 19th century.

First, some historical background: Wells, Fargo was founded in New York City in 1852 and by July of that year had established an office in San Francisco. Its early business included the transport of mail and parcels, with much impetus coming from the discovery and mining of gold and other precious metals in the West.

In 1853 it opened an office in Hawaii and by 1863 had extended service to the west coast of Mexico by way of a small private steamship line that called at two Mexican ports.

Upon the completion of the Mexico City-Veracruz railroad in 1873, Wells, Fargo opened an office in Mexico City. As an express company, it touted its ability to move mail and packages much faster, and probably safer, than other carriers. Official postal services in those days were erratic or lacking altogether.

For letters, Wells, Fargo prepared its own special franked envelopes. The so-called franks bore distinctive designs, one could almost call them cachets, prominently showing the firm's name and, in most instances, citing the cost of the message service to be provided.

In addition to what Wells, Fargo charged for the franked envelopes, the sender was required to pay the corresponding Mexican postage. In a way, Wells, Fargo acted as forwarders, expediting movement of mail and parcels overland, particularly on the rapidly expanding railroad system. It operated under strict condition of agreements signed with the governments of the United States and Mexico. Evidently, operations in Mexico became so profitable that by the late 1880s Wells, Fargo had agents in most towns and cities along the west coast from the U.S. border to Mexico.

The special Wells, Fargo franks prepared for Mexico service had five denominations: 10c, 15c, 20c, 25c and 30c, corresponding to the various costs of service offered. These were sent to the government printing office where stamps of the correct denominations were printed on the envelopes.

The first Wells, Fargo franks used in Mexico about 1885 had stamps of the Hidalgo Head Medallion series. Figure 158 shows an early Wells, Fargo frank with the 6c Hidalgo Medallion Head. These were replaced in 1886 with the Large Numeral issue.

Different rates applied to mail that Wells, Fargo delivered within Mexico, to the United States or to Europe. In addition to the proper Mexican postage, Wells, Fargo added a line beneath the franking cachet (usually by handstamp) explaining the type of service for which the envelope was to be used. For example, ". . . ½ oz. letters exclusively for the U.S.," ". . . for the U.S. and Mexico" or ". . . for Europe."

When postal rates changed in 1895 and the Transportation issues (Mulitas) were released, envelopes were prepared bearing these stamps. Figure 159 shows an envelope bearing a July 17, 1897, frank with a 10c stamp of the Transportation issue. There also are instances where franks were struck with two postage stamps to pay for higher-rated letters. There is at least one recorded instance where the stamp was struck three times on the envelope.

Wells, Fargo franks make an interesting collection. Not only was there a large variety of usages, but the green cachets were printed in various shades and bore many different instruction lines. Offices frequently made handwritten changes to the values and weights when the postal rates changed or when stocks of franks ran short. Often if the franks were used entirely within Mexico, they served as receipts.

Figure 159. This July 17, 1897, frank has a 10c stamp of the Transportation issue. The handwritten rerating of the frank covers one ounce, or 30 grams. This also is stamped above the frank.

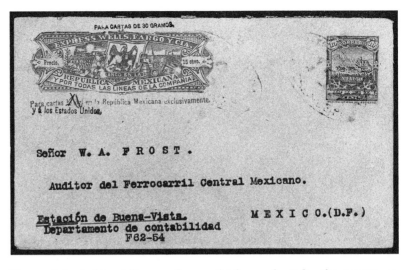

The recipient signed the envelope, which was kept by the agents as proof of delivery. In other instances, multiple franks were used to make up the postage on heavier items. These were affixed to the parcel and were overlapped so the stamp could be canceled. These are called paste-ons. Typically they will not show an addressee, only a handstamp cancellation and sometimes a spot of glue.

Wells, Fargo celebrated the 400th anniversary of Columbus' discovery of America by adding the inscription "1492 * EMISION COLUMBINA * 1892" above its regular frank. This is known as the Jubilee issue.

The year 1892 also marked the formation of two rival express companies in Mexico. These were Express Nacional and Express Hidalgo. Under agreements similar to the one Wells, Fargo had with the Mexican government, these two firms concentrated their activities in an area along the east coast of Mexico between the U.S. border, Mexico City and the port of Veracruz. Their methods of operation were almost identical to those of Wells, Fargo. They used their own distinctive franks and relied heavily on the railroads to carry letters and packages. Both went out of business in 1899. Apparently, they could not compete successfully with the entrenched Wells, Fargo.

Wells, Fargo continued to prosper. When the Mexican government took control of most of the foreign-owned railroads in 1909, Wells, Fargo signed a joint express partnership with the government. In the meantime, it had ceased carrying mail. The latest recorded Wells, Fargo franked envelope is dated September 1907.

Much information is recorded on the Wells, Fargo franked envelopes, particularly in the early issues of *Mexicana*. Another useful source is the Higgins and Gage *World Postal Stationery Catalog*. I frequently see Wells, Fargo covers in dealers' stock, so if you're looking for a new postal history subject to collect, you may want to try this area.

Dead letter covers

If you would like to have some fun with modern postal history, you might want to search for Mexican dead letter covers the next time you're browsing through you favorite dealer's shoe boxes. Several auxiliary postal markings, handwritten endorsements and "rezago" (unclaimed letter) seal labels identify these covers.

Generally, dead letters are inexpensive. They usually are in pretty scruffy condition after all the traveling and handling they have been subjected to. I'm not sure many people understand what they are or are inclined to collect them.

Each cover has its own story. Dead letter covers give interesting insight on the extent to which the postal administration went to track down an addressee or to deliver a letter.

The cover shown in Figure 160 is from the revolutionary period (1914-16), when, as mentioned, there was tremendous civil dislocation throughout Mexico. I'm sure a great deal of mail ended up undeliverable. This item began its journey in Queretaro on August 23, 1914. To assure delivery, a 5c Denver Eagle stamp was added to the 5c stamped envelope, a Federal issue. Perhaps the letter was destined for trouble from the beginning, since the address reads: "Sr. Jose Morales, A Lista de Correo (General Delivery), Puebla, 'urgente.' " This meant that the writer was anxious to contact Morales but did not have the exact address and wanted the letter to be advertised at the main post office in Puebla.

Postal markings on the reverse, also shown in Figure 160, show that the letter passed through Mexico City August 24, was received in Puebla August 26 and was immediately posted on the list for general delivery. This is affirmed by the large circular handstamp inscribed "LISTA/Ago 26 1914/PUEBLA, PUE."

For two months, Morales failed to call at the post office or did not receive notice that his name was on the general delivery list. Once again he was included on the list of October 27, a fact recorded with another strike of the "LISTA" handstamp. When this did not produce results, the face of the letter was marked "NO RECLAMADO" (not claimed), and the letter was turned over to the Dead Letter Office in Mexico City for processing. There, the letter was opened with a slit along the bottom edge. Since there was no return address, the contents were examined for some clue to the identity of the sender. It was determined that a Carmine Martinez was the writer.

The letter was resealed using a stamplike label designed expressly for this purpose. This was affixed across the open slit and received a special "rezagos" cancellation. These ornate postal seals measure about 30mm by 46mm and contain the words "Mexican Postal Service/Officially Sealed/Dead Letter Department" in Spanish. Figure 161 shows a used example of the seal, which naturally is worse for wear, as will be explained shortly.

At that point, the letter was readdressed for return to the sender. This was normally done with red ink on the face of the letter, in this instance between the lines of the original address. Once the letter reached the Queretaro post office, it was again advertised on the general delivery list and so noted with the "LISTA" handstamp of Queretaro (November 8, 1914). Presumably, Carmen Martinez did not expect the letter to be returned, and she did not check the list.

After six weeks, further attempts at delivery were abandoned. The letter was marked, again on the face, "CUMPLIDO" plus a datestamp of the Queretaro office (December 21, 1914). This meant that all provisions of the regulations concerning attempted delivery had been complied with. The letter was then returned to the Dead Letter Office, where the contents were removed, breaking the original seal, and destroyed. In theory, envelopes were supposed to be destroyed, too. Obviously many weren't, and eventually, they found their way into the stamp market.

The three numerical notations on this cover probably relate to the various lists on which it appeared or perhaps a log book. All my dead letter covers have numbers of one sort or another.

Figure 160. The front of this dead letter shows cancellations of August 23, 1914, when the letter was mailed, and December 21, 1914, when efforts to deliver it ceased. Each "LISTA" marking on the back of the cover indicates when the letter was advertised. The seal was used after the letter was opened to try to identify the sender.

I have described the travels of but one dead letter. There are numerous variations, and some can turn into very interesting puzzles. There is a broad range of types of markings that can be found on dead letters. The "LISTA" markings are similar in design and were struck in blue or purple ink. "Rezagos" is another word regularly stamped on dead letters. Handstamps indicating directory service at the various post offices also are quite common.

Attempted delivery often resulted in curious notations by individual letter carriers: "No hay numero" (no such number) and "No esta" (not here) are only two examples.

I have another dead letter that bears an ornate pointing-finger handstamp containing the Spanish words for "Return to Sender" and instructions to check the local directory and then advertise. This letter was opened and resealed twice, once with the label described earlier and the second time with a crude label used by the local post office.

Figure 161. A used example of the ornate postal seals used by the Dead Letter Office.

Conclusion

When first approached by *Linn's Stamp News* to write a monthly column on the stamps of Mexico, I experienced some trepidation. But, at the urgings of several friends, including one outstanding student of Mexican philately, I undertook the task and soon found it was not as daunting as first imagined. Actually, it gave me a great deal of satisfaction knowing I was helping promote a hobby that has given me so much pleasure. Little did I realize then that almost 10 years later I would be asked to transform that monthly series into a book. This was truly an exciting and flattering result of that decision.

In my first *Linn's* column on Mexico in May 1983, one of the themes I emphasized was my feeling that Mexico, as a collecting entity, offered something for everyone. There is such depth and diversity in the philately of Mexico that virtually anyone — beginner, intermediate or advanced collector — could find a niche that would provide intellectual challenge and hours of pleasure in the pursuit of a specific interest. Hopefully, the previous six chapters have given reasonable proof of that premise. They represent a well-mixed (and newly revised) sampling of perhaps a third of the columns published in *Linn's* between 1983 and 1992.

From the beginning, it was my intent to explore as many aspects of Mexican philately as possible. I knew my *Linn's* audience would soon tire of a constant dose of the classic issues, which was my collecting focus. As it turned out, the *Linn's* column forced me into more serious study of areas I had neglected, especially the stamps of the 20th century. These I found to be just as fascinating as the older material.

Another point I made in that inaugural article was that Mexican philately was blessed with a great deal of good literature to guide the beginner and would-be specialist. And perhaps as a contrasting corollary, that there were plenty of areas in Mexican stamps that had not been thoroughly explored, which offered ample opportunity for original research. Both situations continue today. Several basic reference works, many of which are mentioned in the text, have been updated, or substantially added to. Also, new works have appeared on obscure subjects. An example is Karl Schimmer's study of the Porte de Mar stamps, published by MEPSI in 1987, which unraveled some of the mystery of those strange adhesives, as well as providing a much needed review of maritime mail practices of that era. Other authors are currently working on specialized studies that, once published, will add still more light to our understanding of Mexican philately.

As an instance of philatelic evolution, the Mexico Exporta definitive issues, which are dealt with at length in Chapter 4, continue to absorb the attention of scores of collectors, as well as dealers and album makers. In 1983, there were but five or six Exporta issues and perhaps a couple of hundred varieties with which to contend. Now, there are double that many issues and well over 500 varieties to challenge a collector striving for completeness. Few other countries can boast a definitive issue of such philatelic breadth and complexity. The Architecture and Archaeology series of definitive stamps that preceded the Mexico Exporta stamps is another group receiving more attention now than it was when I initiated the Mexico column.

A final observation I offered readers of that inaugural article was the value of belonging to a specialist group in one's field of collecting, in this case the Mexico Elmhurst Philatelic Society International (MEPSI). As a MEPSI member for more than 25 years, I can't tell you how much this association has helped me in the logical and prudent development of my collection. I realize many collectors are wary of joining societies or groups, especially ones that publish and circulate lists and collecting interests of members as MEPSI does. Often this leads to unwanted publicity and unsolicited overtures to purchase philatelic material. But this has almost never happened in my years with MEPSI. On the contrary, I might have expected more. The society is very discreet with its membership records. The few times non-members have been permitted access, it has been for a worthwhile cause. The pluses of MEPSI membership far outweigh any minor negatives there might be.

In the nine years I have been writing the *Linn's* column, many people (including my very patient and supportive wife) have asked where I get ideas. The basic question is: How can I keep going on and on about the stamps of just one country. There have been well over 100 columns since May 1983, with only a few instances of rehashing earlier subject matter. At the beginning, I made a long list of topics I knew something about and had reference material on, which I thought might make good stories. After the column ran for a few months, I realized that letters from readers contained inquiries that could be developed into other new columns. Many times these inquiries required research in areas unfamiliar to me. This, too, spawned new ideas for articles. Also, readers frequently included photocopies of covers from their collections, which produced the same result. And whenever I attended stamp show bourses, I searched the stock books and cover boxes not only for items to fit in my own collections and exhibits, but also for items that might form the basis for another good story in *Linn's*. So far, the well of ideas has not gone dry, and the original list I made still contains a few unaddressed topics.

After almost 30 year of specializing in Mexico, I remain just as excited as ever about its collecting possibilities and opportunities. It's my earnest hope that I have been able to transfer, through my *Linn's* columns and through this book, some of my enthusiasm to collectors who might be searching for an area in which to specialize. To you who are on the verge of adopting Mexico as your special interest, I would say, Do it! We welcome you with a big "abrazo," the traditional Mexican hug of greeting.

Finally, heartfelt thanks are owed to many people who, in a very real way, contributed to my success in keeping the series going. First, there are the loyal readers who took time to write letters of encourage-ment and who offered further insight on the subject matter of the articles. Some have received mention in the text presented. I wish there were space to acknowledge them all. Collector and dealer friends have also provided much input over the years. They have always been willing to search their collections and files for answers to elusive questions. This unselfish sharing among friends (many of whom have never met face to face) has always struck me as one of the hallmarks of our hobby.

If there were to be a dedication of this book, I would have to single out three Mexico collector friends, all now deceased, who helped me most over the years: Jim Beal, who shared his incredibly vast knowledge about Mexican stamps both genuine and forged; John Bash, who, as my auction agent, taught me about the Mexican stamp market; and Herbert Strauss, whose eye for beauty and for the unusual helped steer me to some of the finest Mexican pieces I own. These men typify the friends one makes in this hobby. I feel fortunate to have known them and think they would approve of this small effort to help perpetuate interest in the fascinating stamps of our neighbor to the south.

Appendix

Exporta Definitives

This checklist is arranged for 10 major issue groupings. Recent varieties that some experts have tentatively assigned to an 11th or 12th category have been noted, but there is insufficient evidence to know whether these will become major issues.

Many dealers who specialize in Exporta stamps organize their stocks according to these groupings, and at least one specialized album layout (Lighthouse) also follows this approach. However, there is no guarantee that this list is complete or absolutely accurate. It represents a best effort to present concisely a large body of information from many sources.

How to use the checklist

First, attempt to separate Exporta stamps into the various issues according to the characteristics of paper, gum, and ultraviolet-light response defined in the notes at the end of the tables. Once the stamps are separated into the issue groupings, you can check for denomination, colors, size and perforation varieties. A dot (•) means a stamp exists for the cited characteristics. The number following the dot indicates major color varieties reported. There are many other subtle shades for those with keen color perception. Other letters are explained at the end of the tables.

Surface-mail stamps

| Stamp | Description | Colors | Perf | Width (mm) | Issues (Papers) — See Notes | | | | | | | | | |
					1	2	3	4	5	6	7	8	10 A	B
0.50	Steel Pipe	gry. bl.	14	37.5	•									
0.20	Chemicals	bk.	14	37.5	•	•			•	•				
0.40	Coffee	brn., etc.	14	37.0	•2									
0.50	Auto Parts	bl., bk., etc.	14	37.0	•	•2	•	•	•	•				
0.80	Cattle	car.	14	37.0	•2	•2			•	•				
0.80	Cattle	car.	11x11+	37.0	•3	•2	•x	•						
0.80	Cattle	car.	11.5x11+	37.0			•	•						
1.00	Electric Cable	bl., org.	14	37.5	•	•3		•	•4	•	•			
1.00	Electric Cable	bk., org.	14	36.0							•			
2.00	Abalone	grn., bl.	14	37.0	•2	•2		•	•2	•				
2.00	Abalone	grn., bl.	14	36.5					•					
2.00	Abalone	grn., bl.	14	36.0							•			
3.00	Shoes	brn., etc.	14	37.0	•2	•3	•3	•2	•	•	•3			

Stamp	Description	Colors	Perf	Width (mm)	1	2	3	4	5	6	7	8	10 A	10 B
3.00	Shoes	brn.	11.5x11+	37.0					•	•	•			
4.00	Tiles	brn., tan	14	37.0		•2			•2	•	•2	•		
5.00	Minerals	gry. ol.	14	37.0	•2	•2		•2	•	•				
5.00	Minerals	gry. ol.	11.5x11+	36.0					•		•2	•2		
6.00	Steel Pipe	ver.	14	36.0					•	•				
6.00	Steel Pipe	ver.	11x11+	36.0							•y			
6.00	Steel Pipe	ver.	11.5x11+	36.0					•	•	•			
6.00	Steel Pipe	gry.	11.5x11+	36.0							•2	•		
7.00	Overalls	bl.	14	36.0							•2			
8.00	Overalls	khaki	11x11+	36.0							•			
8.00	Overalls	khaki	11.5x11+	36.0							•2			
9.00	Overalls	dk. bl.	14	36.0							•2			
10.00	Tequila	dk. & lt. grn.	14	36.5	•	•2	•		•	•	•3			
10.00	Tequila	dk. & lt. grn.	14	37.5								•		
10.00	Cattle	car.	14	36.5								•		
15.00	Honey	brn. & yel. brn.	14	36.0							•2	•		
20.00	Wrought Iron	bk.	14	37.0	•	•2		•	•	•				
20.00	Wrought Iron	bk.	14	36.5				•2			•	•		
20.00	Wrought Iron	bk.	14	36.0					•	•				
20.00	Wrought Iron	bk.	14	35.5					•2					
20.00	Wrought Iron	bk.	11.5x11+	35.5								•		
20.00	Bicycle	org., bk.	14	36.5								•		
25.00	Copper Vase	copper	14	33.5							•			
35.00	Books	car., yel.	14	36.0							•			
40.00	Books	brn., yel.	14	36.0							•			
40.00	Books	aqua, gold	14	36.0							•			
50.00	Jewelry	vio., silver, bk.	14	37.0		•	•							
50.00	Books	bl., yel.	14	36.0					•2	•	•2	•		
50.00	Tomatoes	red, grn.	14	36.5								•		
50.00	Tomatoes	red, grn.	14	36.0									•	
60.00	Shoes	brn.	11.5x11+	37.0							•2			
70.00	Copper Vase	copper	14	33.5							•			
70.00	Copper Vase	copper	11.5x11+	33.5							•			
80.00	Books	car., gold	14	36.0							•2			
80.00	Overalls	bl.	14	35.5							•			
90.00	Abalone	grn., bl.	14	36.0							•2			
100.00	Coffee	dk. brn.	14	36.0								•	•	
100.00	Coffee	dk. brn.	11.5x11+	37.5							•			
100.00	Strawberry	car., grn.	14	35.5					•	•	•b	•b		
200.00	Citrus Fruit	yel., grn.	14	35.5					•	•				
200.00	Citrus Fruit	yel., grn.	14	35.0			•				•z	•2z		
300.00	Autos	bl., red	14	36.0			•		•	•	•z	•b		•
400.00	Electronics	yel., brn.	14	36.0							•b	•b		
450.00	Electronics	yel., vio. rose	14	35.5			•							
450.00	Electronics	yel., vio. rose	14	36.0									•	
500.00	Cotton	ol. grn., org.	14	36.0							•b	•b		

Stamp	Description	Colors	Perf (mm)	Width	1	2	3	4	5	6	7	8	10 A	10 B
500.00	Valves	gry., bl.	14	36.0									•	•
500.00	Valves	gry., bl.	14	35.5									•	
600.00	Jewelry	vio., gry., bk.	14	37.0				•						
600.00	Jewelry	vio., gry., bk.	14	36.5								•		
600.00	Jewelry	vio., gry., bk.	14	36.0									•	•
700.00	Movie Film	grn., red, bk.	14	35.5								•	•	•
750.00	Movie Film	grn., red, bk.	14	35.5									•	
800.00	Tiles	brn., tan	14	36.0								•	•	
900.00	Auto Parts	bk.	14	36.0								•	•	•
950.00	Auto Parts	indigo	14	36.0				•					•	
1,000.00	Farm Machinery	dk. red, bk.	14	36.5	(See 9th issue below)								•&	•&
1,100.00	Minerals	dk. gry.	14	37.0									•&	
1,300.00	Strawberry	red, grn.	14	37.0				•					•&	•&
1,400.00	Chemicals	bk.	14	36.0									•	•
1,500.00	Copper Vase	tan	14	33.5									•	•
1,600.00	Steel Pipe	ver.	14	36.0									•	•
1,700.00	Tequila	dk. & lt. grn.	14	37.5									•	•
1,900.00	Abalone	grn., bl.	14	37.0									•	•
2,000.00	Wrought Iron	bk.	14	36.0	(See 9th issue below)							•	•&	•b
2,100.00	Bicycle	org., bk.	14	36.0									•&	•b
2,500.00	Overalls	cobalt bl.	14	36.0									•&	

Stamp	Description	Colors	Perf	9th Issue Width (mm)
				The so-called 9th issue contains the following six varieties (original printings all had normal (I) burelage):
1,000.00	Farm Machinery	dk. red, bk.	14	36.5
2,000.00	Wrought Iron	bk.	14	36.0
3,000.00	Electric Cable	org., gry. bk.	14	36.0
4,000.00	Honey	yel. org., brn.	14	36.0
4,000.00	Honey	buff, brn.	14	36.0
5,000.00	Cotton	grn., org.	14	36.0 (1992 variety: no fibers or watermark; UV active; dry gum)

Airmail stamps

Stamp	Description	Colors	Perf	Width (mm)	1	2	3	4	5	6
0.30	Copper Vase	bronze	14	37.0	•2					
0.50	Electronics	yel. & reddish brn.	14	37.0		•				
0.80	Overalls	dull bl.	14	37.0	•2					
1.60	Bicycle	bk., org.	14	37.0	•2	•	•	•2		
1.90	Valves	ver., dk. grn.	14	37.0	•2	•				
2.00	Books	ult., gold	14	37.0	•2				•	•
2.50	Tomatoes	ver., grn.	14	37.0		•2				
4.00	Honey	brn, yel. brn.	14	37.0	•	•		•		
4.30	Strawberry	pink, ol.	14	37.0	•					
5.00	Autos	dk. bl., ocher	14	37.5	•	•		•		

Stamp	Description	Colors	Perf	Width (mm)	Issues (Papers) — See Notes					
					1	2	3	4	5	6
5.20	Farm Machinery	red, bk.	14	36.5	•					
5.60	Cotton	lt. grn., org.	14	37.0	•					
10.00	Citrus Fruit	grn., yel. grn.	14	36.5		•				
20.00	Movie Film	bk., red, grn.	14	37.0			•2			
50.00	Cotton Thread	cerise, etc.	14	37.0			•		•	

Key:

x = There are two perforation varieties: big holes and small holes.

y = Small-hole perforations

b = Burelage found on stamp in normal orientation (I), arc pointing lower right.

z = Burelage found on stamp inverted (II); arc points to upper left.

& = Stamp is found both with (normal, I) and without burelage.

Paper and gum characteristics — keys to proper identification

1st issue: (1975-79) Glazed phosphorescent-chalk-surfaced Hi-Brite paper (0.09mm), unwatermarked, with glossy dextrin gum, either white or ivory in color.

2nd issue: (1979-81) Thick, glazed, phosphorescent-chalk-surfaced Hi-Brite paper (0.10mm), watermarked "MEX-MEX" plus eagle (Scott 300) with dull PVA, ivory-colored gum.

3rd issue: (1981-89) Thin, unglazed onionskin paper, fluorescent throughout (0.08mm), unwatermarked with glossy dextrin gum. High values are the late 1989 printings.

4th issue: (1981-83) Thick, phosphorescent-chalk-surfaced Hi-Brite paper (0.10mm), unwatermarked, with dull white to cream-colored PVA gum.

5th issue: (1982-84) Thin, glazed Hi-Brite paper (0.08mm), with dull PVA gum. The paper is fluorescent-chalk coated on the face only.

6th issue: (1982-84) Same as the 5th issue except the paper is fluorescent-surfaced on both the face and reverse of the stamps. The gum is white.

7th issue: (1984-85) Medium thick (0.09-0.10mm) Hi-Brite paper, with very bright fluorescence on the face. Unwatermarked with dull, cream-colored PVA gum.

8th issue: (1985-87) Same as the 7th issue except the paper is slightly more opaque (non-translucent) and measures 0.10mm.

9th issue: (1988) A non-active, thick granite paper (0.11mm) with embedded blue rayon fibers. Watermarked "MEX-MEX" plus eagle (Scott 300) with glossy, ivory-colored dextrin gum. Watermark is difficult to see except on selvage.

10th issue: (1989-91) Thick, glazed, unwatermarked paper (0.11mm) with dull, ivory-colored gum that may appear faintly ribbed (H) under oblique light. Two light-active subgroups are recognized: "A" — early printings on totally non-luminescent paper; "B" — paper with spotty, low-level luminescence owing to the presence of optical brighteners. Fluorescent inks also were used, which change color and intensity under ultraviolet light.

Notes:

Colors: The following is a list of abbreviations for colors used in the listings. There are literally dozens of shades, and it would be impossible to describe all of them. The following are the general colors most frequently encountered:

bl. = blue	dk. = dark	org. = orange
bk. = black	grn. = green	ult. = ultramarine
br. = bright	gry. = gray	ver. = vermilion
brn. = brown	lt. = light	vio. = violet
car. = carmine	ol. = olive	yel. = yellow

Perforations: The vast majority of Exporta stamps are perforated 14. Those collectors with exceedingly precise perforation gauges will find that the varieties may measure slightly different from the combinations noted; i.e., 14 x 14.25, 11 x 11.25 and 11.5 x 11.25. A "+" is used for increments less than 0.5mm.

Width: The width measurement is the width of the design, including the imprint. For multicolored stamps wherein the same color is not encountered on both edges, the design width may vary as much as 0.5mm because of imperfect color registration. Examples would be the 1.90p Valve stamps of the 1st issue airmail stamps.

Paper: Viewed under ultraviolet light, subtle color and fluorescent differences will be noted for papers in the same issue groupings. They are the result of imperfect control of optical brighteners used in the manufacture of these papers. Some lists attempt to categorize these minor differences, but it is not done here. The paper thickness noted in the descriptions includes gum. Soaked, off-cover stamps may be particularly difficult to assign to the proper groupings. Not only will their thickness be slightly less than that listed, but light-sensitive properties may have been altered by contact with water. Longwave ultraviolet light (3,000-4,000 angstroms) works best with these stamps.

Burelage: High denominations of issues 7, 8, 9 and 10 have been printed on paper bearing patterns of closely spaced curved lines as a security measure. The patterns are found with two orientations: (I) with the top of the arc pointing towards the lower-right corner of the stamps, and (II) the top of the arc towards the upper left. Dots followed by a "b" denote varieties that have burelage in the normal orientation (I). Those with a "z" have type II orientation. Dots followed by "&" are varieties that occur both with and without burelage.

Index